The Undiscovered Country

W · W · NORTON

JOHN HAY

The Undiscovered Country

& COMPANY · NEW YORK · LONDON

Grateful acknowledgment is made to The Living Wilderness and The Cape Naturalist
for sections of this book which appeared in their pages.

The text of this book is composed in V.I.P. Janson, with display type set in typositor
Willow. Composition and manufacturing are by the Maple Vail Book Manufacturing
Group. Drawings are by David Canright. Book and binding design by Antonina Krass.

Library of Congress Cataloging in Publication Data
Hay, John, 1915–
The undiscovered country.

1. Natural history.   2. Man's place in nature.   I. Title.
QH45.5.H38   1982   508   81–22276
ISBN 0–393–01571–8   AACR2
ISBN 0–393–30015–3 (pbk.)

W. W. Norton & Company, Inc. 500 Fifth Avenue, New York, N.Y. 10110
W. W. Norton & Company Ltd., 37 Great Russell Street, London WC1B 3NU

1 2 3 4 5 6 7 8 9 0

For Susan, Kitty, and Charles, and their worlds of children, books, music, and architecture, with love

We carry with us the wonders we seek without us: There is all Africa and her prodigies in us; we are that bold and adventurous part of Nature, which he that studies wisely learns in a *compendium* what others labor at in a divided piece and endless volume.

SIR THOMAS BROWNE
Religio Medici

Contents

Foreword

"Nature," a Maine man told me the other day, as we were discussing the weather, "is better than advertising," by which I took him to mean that advertising is not noted for its truthfulness. Surely, we have been surrounding ourselves with too many substitutes for the truth and the reality, creatures prone to fantasy though we undoubtedly are. It also seems like far too much of a burden on science to turn over all the interpretation of nature to it, and a desertion of the inheritance in ourselves. The truth lies close to every individual and is at the same time much vaster in scale than we choose to recognize. We have been narrowing down the world to our careless treatment of it, and to those aspects of life and creation that we choose to confine to our definitions. The results are obvious. Estrangement from that whole in which there is no distinction between man and nature is our modern agony. Indifference and brutality have brought about a state of affairs in which we have to struggle to find our place in an "environment" that has replaced the earth itself, spending endless time arguing about where the human race belongs. As a result of acting like outsiders, we find to our alarm that we are turning into predators who are in danger of losing their prey, territorialists who are running out of territory.

It is my own thought, giving all due credit to an amateur pursuit of natural science that gave me the extra directions I needed, that science, though our major explorer, is not enough. We never really live with the greater world of life until we admit it into ourselves. That implies recognition of the supreme innocence in which we and all other beings were nurtured, and of that ongoing experience, surpassing itself, to which every life is exposed. In other words, during our lifetimes, we share in the unendingly changing facets of the sentient earth; and it seems useless to discriminate on behalf of those who might be better suited to that companionship than others. The universe, not human society, will see to that. We were born into the great democracy of nature, no matter how far we seem to have strayed, and more and more people are looking for ways to be its citizens again.

A new relationship between us and the living world is still ahead of us, in what form no one can say. Who knows how the infinitely complex relationships of the watery planet will realign themselves tomorrow? It will not be entirely of our doing. Order as we see and impose it is more circumscribed than the springs of universal variety. But we have to begin with a commitment. The mysterious terms of existence, which are not printed in our reports, are found in our everyday lives. We may not know ourselves well enough to understand why we behave the way we do, but we receive the universe directly. The surest way ahead is to trust the primal source that each life, human or nonhuman, embodies. Coexistence requires love, and at the very least an acknowledgment that we do not live in isolation. The exploration has hardly started.

PART ONE

Dimensions of the Past

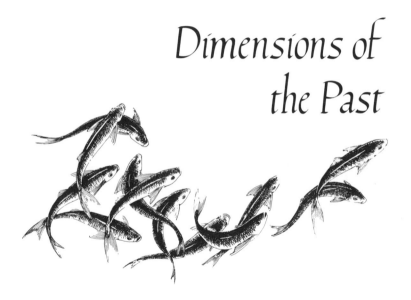

CHAPTER 1

The New World

". . . a plain wilderness as God first made it."

CAPTAIN JOHN SMITH

I was an outsider, coming back to a country I had been born in but had hardly been given enough time to know. So were we all, displaced persons after a period of war that had engaged the entire globe. It had been an apocalyptic separation from the sun and rain, from all the timeless rhythms that brought back the birds and the sweet spring colors on the trees, that kept the low waves rippling along the shore.

One day I watched the sun setting over the water and listened to the wailing gulls, with no sense that having moved to this place I was really planted anywhere. I felt permanently uprooted, the subject of a civilization that had discovered how to circumnavigate the earth in an instant and almost how to circumvent all the exactions of nature. We had learned how to blast our way through life and death, although we seemed to have very little idea of how to deal with the consequences.

I was stranded on the beach, the victim of an age that consumed its own history, part of the tidal wrack and litter flung in from all points of the compass. Despair took me. I flapped on the sands like a fish out of water. "Hold on. Help is not coming."

Who was I? Where did I live? One night I dreamt that the house we had newly built, perched on an inland ridge overlooking Cape Cod Bay, was floating out in the middle of the ocean like a raft, with storm waves breaking over it, and the floor leaking. All the new highways then being constructed did not seem to lead me anywhere, but confined me to islands between them, waiting to hitch a ride. The seasons might have been reduced to unseen intervals, dates on a mechanical calendar. How and where should I start again, facing this monotonous, windswept plain, with no guidance? The sea was wonderfully indifferent to my complaints.

One cold and windy day, I stood on the wharf at Provincetown watching a dragger unload its catch. As the crew sorted out and cleaned the cold, slippery bodies of cod, haddock, and flounder, their hands were meat red. The white fish skeletons were the leavings of a vaster appetite than even fishermen knew, and the gulls, practiced for ages in this kind of trade, were wheeling and crying overhead. So it had been for thousands of years: the original exercise, the inescapable condition. And although our age seemed to have cast itself out beyond all moorings, this was where the New World came into view again.

From where we lived, our eyes swept down over the tops of oaks and pitch pines until they met the circle of the bay, a kind of great bowl of seawater investing the contours of the land. At low tide, sandy flats extended for nearly a mile out toward the last retreat of the waves. It was a wide, elastic range exposed to all the weather, every extreme of temperature and condition throughout the year. The watery shallows swept across tan-colored sands covered by ripples made by wavelets during the advance and retreat of the tides. Some sections were made up of a mosaic of short, curling wavelike forms, and others had long, fluted, undulating avenues crossed here and there by bird tracks. Everything suggested travel, sweeping away, sweeping back in again. The waters pulled outward toward the depths, and, as part of a global exercise, periodically turned to rise toward the shore.

When I walked out over the flats, to stay there at times for as long as several hours before the tide turned and sent me inland again, the life forms schooling or twitching in the depths beyond were not only hidden. I had very few names to give them. And the endless tracks over the sand, the innumerable little holes, the castings, and the debris of weed and shells with the many lives that attached themselves to it belonged to another kingdom I had only begun to be aware of. It was a first opening into original space. In the sense that I was largely ignorant of what to call its occupants, it was a mystery. On the other hand, I saw that it was also ours, the neglected space in ourselves.

When you stand on the beach, you can see about five and a half miles out to the horizon, before the round world seems to drop off. On ocean voyages, it is a matter of moving over the earth's curve, checking your course as you go. Before I became aware of these facts, I remember traveling to England on a small liner at the age of seven. I remember an endless range of waves, rocking in deep green, stomach-sinking troughs; I saw rolling plains of ebony, lead, quicksilver, gold, and jade, swelling and heaving under the sky. Now and then I caught sight of a roving seabird; now and then a roving rain lanced down through the cloud countries overhead. I sensed that ocean travel, all the way around the world, meant a moving-on-forever, over the backs and flanks of the waves, up and down, not lost, but out the other side—an outward passage such as a child could take for granted.

So, in this country, by the sea, I looked to that other side again, as if I could leap all the intervening years and accept the first, nameless condition where death and life are held in one. This oceanic anonymity had called forth fear since the world began, but it reached for me. And as I followed the flats out, jumping their ribs and lanes, I felt they might lead me to any number of countries I had never known before.

The tide was the framework that governed the shorebirds, crabs, gulls and clammers, and other people I met out there meandering, circling in the right proportion, as if to discover and be discovered. We could not escape it. All the same, in spite of their recurring, accurate rhythms, tides crossed time. They certainly had only a passing connection with my watch, which was geared to the great business of the human world, and they ignored the modern obsession with being in such a rush—to what end? I could see that if you wanted to understand the action of the tides you probably had to start by slowing time down, so that an hour became a day, a day a century. So I kept watching those graceful, inexorable turnings. On the incoming tide, I stood in the water as it began to trickle in, with bubbles and foam on the tidal lips, a filmy sheet transporting fine grains of sand and light debris, running between the ripple marks that braided the sands. As the water deepened, small bunches of rockweed attached to isolated rocks and stones began to lift their golden skirts, and thin, green ribbons of eelgrass floated and streamed like weather vanes in the direction of the shore. These great repetitions gave me another lease. They opened life to the enigma of beginnings. What was the real power, under our global pretensions, that ran the year?

Wandering, over the sands and inland across the bubbling marshes, and into the woods and thickets, became a way of seeing. "Man has but a dim light in him," says St. Augustine; "let him walk, lest darkness overtake him." But only to walk in a straight line, even for Christian reasons, is not necessarily the best way to travel. Fish, gulls, and weather circle on, in the endless process of becoming, and through that motion we discover the unexpected, which we might otherwise pass by.

My new neighborhood was not just the countryside, which our society sees with dominating eyes and determines to change for its own good, but a land, or lands, of the universe, peopled by lives that came to the present out of unrecorded time. Out on the flats, and no less inshore, I could expose myself to currents of unfailing energy, while light and water kept flowing past, and feel a wealth of other senses moving with me. Every life was taking advantage of its time. In learning to recognize these members of a greater community, not only by their labels, as objects of natural history, but for their connections with myself, I started to make some progress. I pushed out the boundaries that had confined me, and it began to be an open world again.

CHAPTER 2

The Home Stream

It was clear to me that I had unfinished business with the past, which I had left too soon through no fault of my own, and that I needed better guidance toward the future. Luckily I had some unexpected help from neighbors, both human and, just as important, fish, who began to head me in the right direction. After many tentative steps and a nibbling around the edges of possibility, I began to walk, as St. Augustine suggested, and found some leaders in the new country that I could never have imagined only a short time before.

The town landing at Paine's Creek, from which you can walk down to the beach and then over the sands on the ebb tide, has a tidal creek running by it, scalloping its banks, which merge with the salt marshes behind. Still further inland, the stream, as Stony Brook, starts to climb upward toward a series of freshwater ponds. It was in these waters that I first saw the alewives, or freshwater herring (*Alosa pseudoharengus*), that run in out of saltwater along the Atlantic coastline to spawn during their spring migration, meeting their enemies the herring and black-backed gulls that cruise along the shore at all times of the year. So inexorably serious were they, so perfect in their motion, so far-reaching was their journey in its implications of how little we know of other lives in nature, that I had to follow them. I smelled them on the water. I started walking the banks of the stream to look for them, down its entire length. I watched their forward-staring eyes. I heard the gulls shouting over them, and I began to realize, as they worked their way upcurrent, that there was more than one way of finding home.

The alewives moved in to Paine's Creek on a tide where there was enough water to swim in, sometimes at night, but often in their full migratory force and numbers during the day, when gulls occasionally caught hundreds or thousands as they swam in on an outgoing tide, to their extreme cost. A few entered as early as March, but the big runs occurred after mid April. I found that they had a circling motion as they moved upstream, within the greater circle of coming in from deep water and returning after they spawned, which was characteristic of other schooling fishes, as well as flocks of birds, not to mention the circle of the seasons within the year, and by collective inference, the lives of men.

Early spring, then as now, is the time when the bay waters begin to change color, from winter gray to a blue-green, and offshore waters coming in over the shoals and sandbars a mile out show long lines of white as they are whisked and turned to spray, maned by the wind. It is Advent season again, a tricky, shifting time of light, The birds sing, fall silent, fly urgently from place to place. Predawn stars sparkle through the waking trees. The still waters tremble in the marsh ditches where killifish flit across their muddy beds. The light falls through the gray, still leafless oaks in a silvery rain, a shifting of secrets, hinting at new life to our hibernating senses. We move out, yawning and complaining as usual, into a land of magic transformations.

Those early, mercurial days brought in forms so new to me as to seem abstract. The first swallow flew in from the South, hurriedly beating its way upwind just offshore. The atmosphere over the blond marshes was cool and gray, heavy with moisture from the sea, and when the sun shone obliquely through, the saltwater might be almost glassy calm, a white fog shining over it in hills of its own, so that an offshore fishing boat looked suspended on a height. When the cool, intermittent showers struck soil and new grass it made a slightly acrid smell. Spring led me toward realms without a name, where the gnats rose through the air, glassy zooplankton danced in saltwater, where the great fish circled offshore waiting for the right conditions to enter the land. Perhaps they were at last leading me toward the mysteries of where I ought to be.

There is such a multitude of fish moving upstream during the spawning season, even in these days of declining populations, that although you felt little interest in them you could never mistake it for a minor phenomenon. In fact, it moves many people to wonder why it should occur at all, as if they were suddenly aware of an equivalent force and motivation in themselves that were still only dimly understood. And it often drives them to start asking questions. I tried to get more information about this migration, not only from the fisheries people and what marine scientists I could find who knew something about it, but also from the town alewife warden, who held one of the oldest offices in America. To talk to Harry Alexander was to talk to an older New England that has almost disappeared, though you can never predict the deeper influences shaping those who live long enough in a place to be able to call it their own. In fact, an endangered species is a definition of human beings dispossessed of their environment. Harry, in any event, was *there*, an intrinsic part of the herring run, and even if his information was not always accurate it was authentic enough, for that reason.

When I think of him, "down country" in Massachusetts from the New Hampshire I spent much of my boyhood in, as well as many other New Englanders who had never traveled very far in their lifetimes because they "had no cause to," I remember such elements as white, embroidered curtains on the frosted glass panels of a front door. I remember stars and ferns, after a frosty night, etched on the windowpanes of an old farmhouse; or hissing, blinding snow running past the corner of a barn, which was all I needed to be able to imagine a hundred desperate travelers in direst need. And certain faces come back to me, like those leathery-skinned farmers at the corner store, hardly ever free of winter, with a certain withheld dignity to them, keeping their privations secret from the prying world. I would see them in the spring in New Hampshire, in town to talk after the ice went out of the lake, and imagined they were the ones who knew where all the real storms were. They and their times may be all gone, over and done with, like a gallery of old photographs, but in the stress of the enduring seasons, they are still distinct enough. I see the blue crust on winter fields, the kerosene lamps, the hot stove where the old people sat, the steaming pile of manure outside, the severe parlor waiting for the minister's visit. These people were molded by the earth's inescapable atmosphere. Over the years, the storms and occasional hurricanes beat down and tore into the fields and woodlands. (The hurricane of 1938 made groves of great white pines, like cathedral aisles, groan and fall over like piles of match sticks.) A wife and husband lost everything they owned in a fire; the young danced; the old died; the snow broke down the old barn roof; the droughts were inexorable and the rocks too hard for the human back and spirit. (In the old days there were not too many relaxing amusements for north-country people, by comparison with today; and it might be said that they were not often amused.)

In some respects, life was less pinched in coastal Massachusetts, where you did not have rocks and cold soil to fight but could depend on a quixotic but fertile ocean. Harry Alexander was a shoreline Cape Codder who spent most of his life moving between the tidal flats and his house. He was thickset, and had a large, reddish nose and a speech that carried echoes of seacoast Britain centuries before. Using, some said abusing, his position as chairman of the alewives committee, he commanded the run each spring, dispensing roe to special friends of his, and scaring off unruly children with a roar. (I do not know whether the story is apocryphal or not, but I once heard that his minister father, who was a great, tall man, was traveling across the Cape one day, driving his horse and wagon, when the horse collapsed. So, this giant proceeded to lift the horse into the wagon, get between the shafts, and pull it home himself.) At a time when I was trying to get as much information as I could about the subject, I asked Harry many questions having to do with the alewives, or "herrin'," during the spring migration, and he returned me some outrageous, some useful, and always uncompromisingly human answers.

One day we had a discussion about eels, which lay in wait for the little alewives that were hatched out in the ponds and at some point in their development would let the current take them downstream toward the marshes and Cape Cod Bay. The two species have opposite migrations, the eel being catadromous, spawning in saltwater and growing up in fresh, whereas the alewives were anadromous, spending only a short time in the freshwaters where they lay their eggs. I told him that I had heard the eels spawned and died out in the mid Atlantic, in the region of the Sargasso Sea, and that the little eels, or elvers, starting as larvae, drifted all the way to our coastline, where they entered hundreds of rivers and streams and there matured.

"Now, John," he said "you know that isn't so. They spend their life right here in the brook."

Then I told him what I had heard about it from a marine biologist at Woods Hole. His answer to that was: "You know we've had enough of those scientists." I guess he was thinking about the bomb. In any case, he was not one to stand in awe of science.

He felt that the fish and the brook that took the fry down to the bay were in his personal charge. "Here's the story on that, see. We have to see that the youngsters don't have any trouble getting back after they're hatched out, so there has to be a free flow in the brook. If you don't take care of this stream they'll get into trouble."

He came from a period of piety and impiety, churchgoers and atheists, rum runners and rum drinkers, gull and shore-bird killers, house burners, cussed land owners. As he told me once, talking about a closeness to the earth, which seemed to be losing its hold: "We lived on fish and potatoes. That's why some of us old farts lived so long."

Harry was capable of some harshness and meanness, along with much rascally humor and joviality. You sensed opposite qualities in him, catadromous and anadromous migrations, which might lead in a more complicated personality to genius. He had a son named Kenneth, with whom he drove around in a red pickup truck, a journey that often touched by the packaged-liquor store, both for talk and a means of refreshment. His wife, Jessie, a tall, dark, thin woman who was said to have Indian ancestry and was possessed of a quick temper and a direct sense of humor, was often harassed by her male charges. It was reported that she had to hide her money so as to keep them from the bottle. Once she found that they had secreted the booze under the hood of the truck. It was a losing battle. From the outside, at least, I got hints from time to time of the suppression of furies in that house: old country living, passion in a box.

Kenneth drank too much. He was subject to epileptic fits, and, in his later years at least, looked almost older than his father, sad and red-eyed. But he had been a master mechanic, and there was a gentle and sensitive quality to his nature, which he showed through his gentlemanly manner, and a hesitant, apologetic way of speaking. One day I met him down at the town landing, at a time when his father was in the hospital, a few months before he died. He called me over from the seat of the family pickup and said: "Come closer. I want to tell you something about father."

He told me about Harry's being in the hospital and what his reaction to the ignominy of it had been. "Kenneth," said he, "get me my shoes, which are to home, and my wearing apparel. I want to get the hell out of here." That, it seems to me, belongs with Cleopatra's call to Iras: "Give me my robe, put on my crown. I have immortal longings in me."

As I walked away from the truck, after a little further conversation, Kenneth, in his sad, mad way, said: "I thank you for your kind attention."

Harry was not a learned man. Some called him "King of the Herring Run," though at times he acted more like the Lord of Misrule who was a central figure in the country-village festivals of old England. But in a sense he sent his wards, the "youngsters," ahead of him to educate those of us who came after. It was a simple commitment, but real enough. As I think about him, in this crazily conscious age where anything goes between us and reality, I know there is no substitute for direct exposure. Living with, rather than upon, is where the fundamentals are. Wade into that common stream and you find the uncharted connections beginning to widen from whatever contact you happen to make.

One evening I shone my flashlight down into the water at the outlet of Paine's Creek and saw one of Harry's eels, a wiggling ribbon not more than two to three inches long. It had not arrived on schedule the way robins do on your front lawn. It had materialized. This semitransparent creature, gray-blue by day, a ghostly green in the ray of light, this sliver of life, had taken a year to reach the continental shelf from the Sargasso, where it had hatched from an egg in warm saltwater. The European variety, with much farther to go, takes two and a half. Both species, their beings measured by oceanic rhythms, grow and metamorphose in stages from a larva in the shape of a leaf to the elver, or glass eel. This one, wiggling along the sandy bank, was a survivor. Countless others died along the way. It takes such multitudes to uphold the miracle of life on earth.

The appearance of the elver was as wonderful in its way as the entry of the alewives, which have a tendency, after spending two to three years in the sea at unknown distances, to return at sexual maturity to the same stream where they started to grow up. It is a "home stream," in other words, like no other, recognizable in the senses of a fish, commonly but mysteriously found.

The tiny eel was an apparition, a nothing out of nowhere, so it seemed, like a star in the wind, an exceptional identity out of an anonymous, vast sea, incredibly long earth practices behind it, something fleeting, something lasting, past all our concepts of endurance, as the tidewaters rolled away into the night. I am told that there is a Chinese instrument called the ch'in whose sounds are said to be "the sounds of emptiness," which pervade the universe and set the heart of the player in tune with mystery. So the sight of an elver put me in touch with reaches out of mind.

CHAPTER 3

Within the Tides

The measure of things, in the particular orbit you occupy, can take you a lifetime to pursue, and even then you will not get to the end of it. In fact, having reached a much further point in my life, I am not sure I take in as much as when I first watched the great swordplay of the sun between the oceanic clouds and felt that the world had now begun to be a more possible place to live in. How wild and wonderful it is to be out in open territory with everything to learn! The true beginner knows nothing and meets everything. Isn't that what anyone would want, obeying the pure traveler's instinct, out under the rainbow and the rain, out in the still unclaimed reaches of the earth?

The tidal community I had come to was known to its fish and eels, to crabs, shorebirds and sandworms, as well as the clammers and fishermen who still depended on its cyclical rhythms, but some of the rest of us had to start from scratch. I remember one of the older inhabitants saying that the place was getting filled up with people who did not seem to know where they were. No end of new populations were starting to move in, and sometimes away again almost as soon as they arrived. They tried out the land as no other life could, selling and exchanging, driving in and asking where to go, settling in unsettled. This new exchange society grew like mushrooms after rain. It had not been very long since the days when there were small farmers here, still backed up against the sea, in spite of the human wave that had torn beyond them to level a continent. But the farms were nearly gone by the end of World War II. The rapidity of change had begun to overwhelm the kind of individuality and dialect that relative isolation once fostered. Terms started to be disconnected from the grounds they started with. If you don't know what a black-crowned night heron is, then you don't understand the term "Quok," for the call it makes. This bird, because of its twilight and nighttime feeding habits, was once associated with "ha'nts" and evil spirits. "Sawbelly" was an alewife, because of the teeth, or serrations, on its keel. "Hearty" was an old Cape Cod term referring to the main dish, such as roast beef. So the myths and the realities depart. Where do carrots come from? "Simplify. Simplify," said Henry Thoreau. We have to identify, identify before we can even reach that point.

There might be much to be said against the "old days," when life could be narrow and niggardly, when the land was denuded and the shorebirds shot to near extinction. All hawks were "chicken hawks" and most animals, aside from the domestic breeds, were "varmints." Still you cannot take their sources away from them. The sea was not just a backdrop for exploitation but a profoundly present neighbor; and beyond every kitchen garden was a wealth of space, from shore to distant shore.

One day I talked with the then chairman of the Board of

Selectmen, now "passed on," a man named "Fobey" or "Fobe" Foster, at the town landing. He spoke with a rapid, nasal twang, and his way of speech came from a more closely knit New England than seems evident today. "Isn't it a nice place?" he said, as we looked out over the water at a flock of black ducks rising steeply into the air. One of the "quick-winged birds," he called them. He talked about the Cape as it used to be before the new highway down its spine, land speculation, and itinerant crowds had begun to change it. In those days, he said, you could go picking huckleberries anywhere, no matter whose land it was. Set that off against often jealous and suspicious feelings about boundaries, so that neighbors might not speak to each other for twenty years or more, and it was still an open range where you were free to roam, picking berries to your heart's content, not to mention chasing cows through the scrub in the evening to bring them home, or, as one woman put it, "weaving baskets all the month of May." The New England country world was full of truants not likely to show up in the schoolhouse when they needed to set their traps, or when the springtime liberated the air and fish started to bite in the streams.

L. Thomas Hopkins, the educator, who had his ninety-second birthday in 1981, wrote the following about his boyhood in Truro, when you dug your living from fields that had to be retrieved from sand. "Truro had its lowlands or swamp lands for the gardens to produce the vegetables for summer eating, and for storing in root cellars for winter use. Then there were the few upland locations for potatoes and the white turnips, one of the few cash crops saleable in Boston markets. But in spite of the wind and sandstorms the land furnished wood for heat, vegetables and fruit for food, hay for the horse and cattle with surplus for the hogs, hens, ducks and geese. So as a boy I learned to manage, conserve and enrich it.

"As with the sea, acceptance, kindness, and understanding were the avenues to living together successfully.

"The sea was always a friend around us. Sometimes it was

quiet, peaceful, beautiful. At other times it was like an enraged, roaring monster. But whatever its moods, the people of Cape Cod could not live without it, for the fish it furnished kept them alive."

The sea was still around us, but the older, closer relationships seemed to be slipping away. In spite of the few remaining, longtime residents who could tell me where to find fish in the act of spawning, or suggest ways to locate myself so as to avoid getting lost offshore in the fog, or show me where to dig for clams, I began to see that I might have to look for my directions elsewhere in the future. So I walked down to the shore again from a land that had lost its farms to watch the workers who were still reaping and tilling it. The inspiring shafts of the sun struck down through the cloud canopy to fire the water, and the gulls, wailing and crowding in at the mouth of the creek when the fish came in, were crowned in that exposure. The sea was still in charge of an elemental kindness; its tides had never altered.

What were those tides that rose and fell, determining the daily feeding and resting habits of the fiddler crabs and the gulls? They poured in from the outer horizon and then gradually backed out again, an endless process that I had always been aware of but never really questioned. The explanation of tidal phenomena is not hard to find, but the extent and effect of its local variations had not really occurred to me. Still, it was easy to see that on the north, along Cape Cod Bay, where tides rose to nine feet, the flats and salt marshes were far-reaching, but relatively small on the south side where the tidal range was only two feet. The tides along these shores, are not due to the direct pull of sun and moon because the coastal waters are not extensive enough to develop them. Instead they start as tidal waves generated by astronomical forces out in the deep ocean and move over the continental shelf as free waves. As Dr. Alfred C. Redfield pointed out in a paper on the subject, the difference in tidal range between the two sides of the Cape has to do with a complex matter to the south of interfering tidal waves, differing in time from place to place. On the north, where Cape Cod Bay opens into the Gulf of Maine, the range of the tide increases as it enters this wide embayment, from ten feet at its opening on the Provincetown end to thirty feet at its head in the Bay of Fundy. Tidal currents entering such embayments are checked by the land and slosh up against it, like the water in an enclosed tank or your bathtub.*

Dr. Redfield, a distinguished Cape scientist whose studies were basic to much of the advanced ecological work being done today, used to sit on a campstool watching the salt marshes in his home town of Barnstable, month after month, year after year. He measured the growth of the spartina grasses that pioneer a growing marsh. He probed the depth of peat below them. He watched and measured the tides and their action. He calculated the rise of sea level in recent centuries and estimated the growth of the marsh as it developed along with it. And when it was finished, his study was a classically simple description of how one organic system developed and how rhythmically tuned and balanced it was with the sea that invaded and surrounded it.

The two spartina grasses, the principal plants of the salt marshes, are the *alterniflora*, growing on low marsh areas closer to tidewater and along the tidal creeks, and the finer, smaller *patens*, which grows further in, over level areas of high marsh. Both are complexly adapted to immersion in saltwater over periods of time. Their very particular physiology is the foundation of the marsh. Its peat was made by their decaying roots, and its growth depends on their adjustments to sea level. They are a living measure of time and the sustained equilibrium of the coastal environment.

I reflected that his study, pure science as it was, might have

*"Tide and Time on Cape Cod," by Alfred C. Redfield, from the *Cape Naturalist*, Vol. 1, No. 2, Sept. 1972.

drawn much of its satisfying unity from the fact that the Barnstable marshes had been the author's home. It suggested a calm, selective faculty, an assurance of mind, that must have been born in the free interplay of one place, a place you have in you with which to compare the larger world beyond it. The subject of tides and marshes is complex, and as open-ended in its way as the unseen horizon. The tides can be accurately calculated, but they are of universal systems that are ultimately beyond our understanding. One scientist, at the end of a lifelong study of oxygen, had to admit that he did not really know what oxygen was. Neither I nor the herring gull cruising along the shore could have even touched on such an admission, but insofar as this range could be said to be our home, we had infinite vistas still ahead.

As time went by, I ran into the fact that salt marshes were vulnerable to random and ignorant destruction. It helped me, in joining to fight for their conservation, to have learned something of the order, the unique, precious character of their existence. "Nothing is perfect," said John James Audubon, "but primitiveness." Nothing replaces the universal fitness. We have nothing to match it. Therefore we cannot let it go. To destroy the marshes and the spartina grass, if we are still to be members of this planet, would be to destroy ourselves.

> "A child said *What is the grass?* fetching it to me with full hands.
> How could I answer the child? I do not know what it is any more than he.
> I guess it must be the flag of my disposition, out of hopeful green stuff woven."—from "Leaves of Grass," by Walt Whitman

Out across the flats, like the postglacial landscape it once was, full of shallow pools and silver light, the tidal wave coming in over the Atlantic does its latest turn, on time to the minute. Water trickles shoreward, spreading and deepening over the ribbed sands, and as you stand there you are at the center of a global complexity. Wavelets and rivulets cross each other and separate in an unending variation of patterns. It is a rising, a turning to new uprisings, a major change, a primitivism carried out in order and grace. The tidewaters exchange with fresh and brackish waters out of creeks and marshes; they carry in new material; new food and energy move back and forth, back and forth, maintaining the earth's standards of provision.

Even in our apparent lack of dependence on them, we are never really separated from the tides that are in all of life. The timing of our days is not so exact a matter as the millionth of a second measured by an atomic clock, but moves with the "seamless" wind and the intricate play of light. We live ahead through the play of an indefinite sequence of complex events. Everything lies ready to be, for an instant, a thousand years, and though we may be able to count and measure everything we meet, the great, cosmic swing of the tides takes us beyond all measurement.

CHAPTER 4

The Oldest Place on Earth

Move to a new place, and in time you may develop no more than one routine, one direction, and one return, proving the statement made by William James to the effect that human beings function at only a small percentage of their potential. When I began to stray off the road into neighboring woodlands, abandoned fields, bogs, and thickets I had never entered before, I found spatial opportunities opening up whose existence I had never suspected, as if I had got into the habit of thinking that since the highway beyond our house could get me from there to California or Alaska, I had no need to look any further. That we get stuck in our ruts is hardly news, but it is news that there are still a vast number of unemployed directions waiting for us on an earth we think of as monopolized by our own initiatives. Those original, tidal motions which affect every inch of the globe were never compromised by human occupation, and the communities that go with them and live according to their rules take part in an unending exercise. The fallen logs are riddled with explorers. The soil is clicking, turning, and changing with the energies of a fantastic variety of occupants. The migrants of the air and waters are weaving a network of global relationships that we are hardly aware of. All this might come under the strict heading of natural history and the guides to tracks and holes which I had begun to consult, but it also proved to be an education in dimensions.

Skunk tracks in the snow led me to a hibernating box turtle, which in turn led me to an awareness of slow time. The spider on its web was an engineer who spanned his delicate reaches in terms of a discipline and order that were beyond my grasp. The tracks of migrant shorebirds in the wet sands pointed to societies whose elaborate nature I had never really been aware of before, and hinted, moreover, at the degree to which great hemispheric travels were lodged in the brain of a small bird. And all these spheres within spheres could be found through no better expedient than walking out and looking up at the sky or down at the ground.

At low tide, spring sunlight conspired with the motion of wavelets and cloud shadows to make fish-scale patterns that kept rippling across the golden floor of the sands. Black-bellied plovers stopped, stood still, ran ahead, while newly arrived terns sped past with their dipping, elastic flight, and the heavier gulls soared at their leisure. Walking over this range where nothing stood still, I picked up elements as much as I did objects. The rings on the empty shell of a moon snail, an animal which slowly roams through underwater sands with a great foot that feels for its prey, leaving conspicuous trails behind it, now sent out a contact with the waves of tidal time. The whorls on its round shell made five complete circuits, the bands growing narrower until they reached an apex, where they finished in a little whirlpool. The curvilinear house of the moon snail, with its smooth, ringed surfaces, was a perfect expression of its range. Inner form and outer reach built that entity; at the apex was an exquisite vanishing point that left temporality behind. When I put the empty shell to my ear I heard the long roar of the surf, as if I were an agent for true form and could contain the unending travels of the world.

(I have less than a rudimentary grasp of physics, but there would seem to be a useful parallel to the moon snail in that living cell which the original microscope brought to light and later instruments found to have a structural complexity that no one could have guessed at just a short time ago. The biological processes in a cell keep their form and timing through an inner spiraling, a twisting and turning, a structure that ensures its living future. It is a thing of the mind, the mystery at the apex, the vanishing point. Perhaps we are all funnels in the wind. Perhaps we are climbing a circular staircase toward infinity. Which is as deep as I am likely to get for the time being, until nature takes me further. Life, as I learned through watching migrant fish and birds, and the trees spiraling toward the sun, is always circling. It is the everlasting way.)

The tidelands, as I walked across them, were like concentric silver disks, the tension in them between water, the sand, the substratum, the organisms at their various surface levels being held within the immediate horizon and at the same time spinning off beyond it. And even though all the half-hidden marine life was still as strange to me as some unknown world at the other end of the earth, I knew it as coextensive with myself, because I too had moved from one horizon to another and returned.

When the spring tides (derived from "springing water") comes each fortnight with the new and full moon, the tide has its greatest range, and this is the time to find the big surf (or chowder) clam, seven inches across. When they are dug out at the farthest reach of low tide or left in the open by a careless clammer or a gull, their weight, bulk, and the impeccable whiteness of their shells makes them look as blind and noble as the clouds.

One day, catching sight of a blackened surface of bone showing above the sand, I dug away with my hands in very cold water and uncovered one of the disks from the spinal vertebra of a whale, large enough to be a finback, with blades like airplane propellers. It was black, pitted, being made of quite porous material for buoyancy, but because it was water sodden, very heavy to lift. As I carried it back, I felt a little closer to those majestic and sensitive globe runners, with the ocean currents along their flanks. Surpassing modes of being need surpassing environments.

The tidal grounds, I had learned, were occupied by distinct communities, and quite far out I could see many tips of the tubular cases of parchment worms decorated with white shell fragments, where they showed above the surface. Further inshore the troughs of the ripple marks, the art of waves, forever being erased and redrawn, were full of the tiny, purplish shell fragments of the *Gemma gemma* tribe of clams. Closer to the beach were the periwinkles, leaving pencil-width trails behind them. They are landward-tending animals, which spend as much time in the air as in the water and will die if immersed for too many hours. The troughs were full of other fragments, like fronds of rockweed torn off by storms or attached to stones, or tufts of reddish-brown Irish moss, and under them there were little bow-backed crustaceans jumping and crawling, or slugs of various colors. Some of the stones and shells were coated with colonial bryozoans, or the plantlike filaments of hydroids, a few of these with the tiny, coiled shells of spirorbis worms attached to them, pink as well as white, elegant as flowers.

The sand was everywhere marked by its occupants and travelers, and its watery lanes kept streaming away, diminishing and expanding. Life in the tidelands is full of regional specialists which hold on to their ways of life by various complex means. They have to thrive in an open plain where the temperatures vary from the extreme lows of winter to the highs of the summer months. They are subjected to periodic uncovering, so they have to endure exposure to the air. There are also wide variations in salinity over the flats, which requires cells and tissues to adapt to them, and the response of differing forms to light and water pressure is unendingly elaborate.

I felt when I walked out there that these marine lands must be the oldest places on earth. With the motions of the changing seas, they fluctuated between one great period of earth history and another, flooding parts of a continent and then receding, a vast though gradual expansion of those daily tides that come only to the head of the beach. There were millions of years of both stability and change in a single shell. It was a mercurial kind of range, and perhaps much of its life had that quality, a potential in it to embody an apparent contradiction of forms, like those fantastic slime molds on land that spread over rotting logs. They are composed of an undifferentiated mass of protoplasm that is classified as a plant but creeps ahead, ingesting bits of leaves and bacteria as it goes.

The marine world, much of it unseen by me, and certainly foreign, pushed out the frontiers. Life could be anything, changing to fit an order far wider than our questions, and at the same time had the stability of the tides and followed the circuitry of the planets. The water swirling around the jetty rocks just off the beach was full of tiny organisms twitching and being shifted back and forth by the currents, and I now knew when I saw them that they followed the geologic scale, in which the past as we are aware of it was as transient as our lives.

Dinoflagellates, the minute creatures of the planktonic protozoa, are single-celled, producing food like plants from sunlight, and, at the same time, are able to propel themselves through the water with their whiplike flagella. Next to bacteria, the protozoa are the simplest creatures on earth. They are also the oldest, all plants and animals having derived from them. Some varieties of the dinoflagellates have a resting phase as round spores or cysts, protected by resistant cell walls, in which they have been incorporated into bottom sediments and recovered as fossils. Some local species are consistent with fossil forms in distant parts of the world. The dinoflagellates incubate in these cysts and move out of them into their motile forms during plankton blooms. These changes occur under such rigidly defined conditions of light and temperature that it has been possible to study climatic conditions in the remote past through studying their fossil forms. Here was the living proof, dancing in the seawaters around me, of the staying power of elemental form.

Then, one day, picking up the newspaper, I received further evidence that we lived close to ages of nearly measureless extent.

Bacteria apparently frozen in the Antarctic ice and soil for at least 10,000 years have grown and reproduced in the laboratory, scientists reported today.

The bacteria were found in sediments extracted by drilling downward in permanently frozen ground at depths of several hundreds of feet below the surface. About four or five different bacterial types were found, some of which grew and were reproduced when put in nutrient fluids.

Geologists estimated that the material in the cores was on the surface of the Antarctic continent at least 10,000 years ago, and perhaps as much as a million years ago. This raises the possibility that the bacteria may have been frozen for several hundred thousand years.

In answer to a query by telephone, Dr. Cameron, of the research team, said some of the bacteria were rod shaped, some club shaped; and some spherical specimens of these grew and reproduced in the laboratory.

"We could all see them wiggling when we observed them under the microscope, but conditions were apparently not right for them to grow."

When I read this I heard resurrection verified. I was now both freed and bound, pulsing through half a million years, half-frozen, half-thawed. Did these facts encourage a liberation in human thought? Somewhere in me they were already known.

As the golden flood of spring released the barnacles on the rocks, flicking out their fans, I felt a corresponding tide of pleasure in me. They danced with all those other water-shaped lives so exhaustively studied by biology and escaping it for new interpretations far into the future. As I walked out on another fairly idle expedition, leaning down and picking up forms and fragments, I was, at the same time, delivered from idleness. I could not avoid joining battalions of fish, legions of worms, droves of snails, the creatures of the plankton making their daily, vertical migrations up to the sunlit surfaces, and the scuttling crabs and darting shrimp. I was obligated to their transformations and their desire.

The gulls had been after *Nereis*, the clam worm, which undulates out of its tubelike burrows to feed. There was a bitten-off section of one being shaken by the wind in a shallow pool so that it looked as if its nerves still functioned, and another one, intact on the sands, that started to writhe with a wavelike peristaltic motion when thrown into the water. Insignificant worm? Beautiful, extravagant worm. Its method of locomotion was effected through the parapods—projecting, orange-colored bristles or "gill feet" that lined the sides of its body, responding to alternate contractions and expansions from one to the other so as to produce the worm's rippling motion. It had muscular jaws with which it voraciously attacked clams and other worms, and was a handsome, steely blue and green, tinged with red, showing the colors of the rainbow in the sunlight. When the clam worms spawn during the summer months, their posterior segments swell with eggs and sperm. Males and females leave their burrows during the dark of the moon and swim to the surface, where they shed eggs and sperm and then drop back to the bottom, where their sexual segments drop off, to regenerate later. The eggs develop into planktonic larvae. In other species the body literally explodes during this mating period as the worms swarm at the surface.

In the great interchange of sex and sustenance, the barnacles were rhythmically feeding on the plankton as the tidewaters rose and fell. At low tide, their volcano-shaped shells were tightly shut so as to retain moisture, and when they were covered again the shell plates opened and out came a feathery foot, or feeding structure, made up of abdominal appendages that flickered back and forth, acting like a net. Barnacles, I found, had comblike mouth parts that scraped off the food they ate.

Each one was hermaphroditic. Along a mile of rocky shore, with a far greater population of barnacles than existed here, their production of larvae, sent off free, swimming for a period in which they, like the worms, became a part of the plankton, must have numbered in the billions. Where they covered the rocks they crowded each other out in competition for light and space, looking like human cities, with some of these miniature skyscrapers rearing higher than others. And, like people in the cities, they apparently communicated after a fashion, releasing chemical signals between them.

Productivity in the marine world was staggering. Oysters could produce a hundred million eggs or more, depending on their size, as compared with a mere three million for the soft-shelled clam, and during their blooms the organisms of the plankton were like pollen dust in the air. Marine fertility is what gave rise to the idea of the inexhaustible sea. The fact that we have started to exhaust whole regions of it does not indicate our capacity for domination so much as a weakness of awe-inspiring proportions.

Nothing was spared in the reproductive inventions that keep these multitudes in being. Sea anemones split apart. By a process of fission, of budding off from a single stalk, one animal becomes two, though each one is identical with the other. The common slipper shell manages to combine both sexes, like the barnacle. Though each one starts off as a male, its reproductive tract degenerates, after which it develops into a female or another male. The older males will retain their sex while they are attached to females—often you may see slipper shells stacked on top of each other—but if a male is put by itself it turns into a female. There also seems to be tendency, when a large number of males are together, for some of them to turn into females. Once female, however, they stay that way. This may have the elements of the kind of sex magic we play around with in our fancy, but it has practical implications for marine animals that are unable to move out freely to look for a mate.

After I first learned what they were, I found the black, leathery egg cases of skates at almost any time of the year, where they had been washed up onto the beach. Each of their four corners is hooked, and sticky when fresh so as to help them attach to the bottom, but they are often dislodged by strong currents and stormy seas. Now and then they can be found with yolk and embryo inside. Young common skates take about a year to hatch out, the time it takes them to grow and use up the yolk being proportionate to water temperatures. When they leave the protection of their cases by slipping out one end, they are smooth, white, slick miniatures of the adult form, but semitransparent, so that you can see their internal organs. Pure, mysterious as all embryos are, perfectly functioning, they seem like little white UFOs sliding into sight

out of murky waters. The adults themselves are strange-look-
ing animals, with eyes placed on the sides of their heads, and
with tough, knobby skins. Their fins, an extension of their
flattened bodies, curl and flap like wings as they slip through
the waters in a smooth and supple style. So the skate child,
well-clad spawn of the sea, is protected for as long as possible
and then cast out, with only a fair chance of making it to
adulthood. To be born, for skate or man, is a dark, unfath-
omed event, with oceanic authority.

And for all the information we try to gather, we are only
surface dwellers looking in on an unfamiliar universe. The fact
is always at variance with the unknown. The scientists have to
consult a noncommittal darkness.

One early summer night, near the Fourth of July, I went
down to the town landing for one of my periodic checkups on
the state of shore and weather. All was in a great enclosed
quiet, except for a flowing wind. I could see dark patches of
cordgrass (*Spartina alterniflora*) growing on the peaty banks jut-
ting out from the beach, and then the shallow waters at half-
tide beyond them, now reflecting smoky colors and seeping
silvery washes under the remaining light. It was like a no-man's-
land out there, a dark and primal ground, keeping its primal
secrets. As I walked down the beach away from the landing, I
suddenly heard a bang, followed by a whizzing, whining sound,
and for an alarming instant thought someone must be firing a
gun in my direction. Then a red ball socked up into the sky,
screeching as it went, to fall slowly down before it disinte-
grated.

That rocket was almost spectacular enough to defy the place
it was launched from, an anomaly in nature, and so was the
long slipstream from a jet plane I caught sight of between the
clouds. Our off-earth experiments and detached desires shot
through the atmosphere, while the old tidal grounds stood by,
playing their magic tricks: "Now you see it. Now you don't."

Though you may reap their rewards in the form of fish or clams, the flats are still a hidden environment, governed more by the sea than the land, a place of indefinite boundaries. Their lives in all their floating or creeping forms—the crabs, the transparent shrimp, the teeming creatures of the plankton, the silver fishes and the gray-green elvers—never seem quite definable. They move away from us in tune with other laws into unexplored depths.

On that summer night, though I had been there many times, I was faced with a dark neutrality that could give no single race its answers, and yet included them all. We could go around the globe past the speed of sound and still have to return to this original enigma. We could plaster the surface of the earth with signs saying "Man," but here on the tidal range we faced signatures in the form of tracks, holes, hieroglyphics past counting that were washed away every twelve hours but amounted to a declaration that would outlast us. The marine waters rose and swept the malleable sands clean, and when they receded the tracks and tunnel openings reappeared. Unquenchable energies streamed away across a great territory that everything and nothing could claim as its own. The script was never final.

I began to visit this magical outer horizon almost every day, emerging from my burrow like a woodchuck, not just to count up the birds and the shellfish, but to be open to the timeless opportunities it offered me to see more than I knew how to see. Often it was only the cold, gray Atlantic locking in the shore, but as the year waited so could I. The range was life and not my notations about it; its waters were always reexpressing themselves, and from time to time there were those grand entries like that of the alewives in early spring which helped me move out further toward where I ought to be.

CHAPTER 5

Appetite

W hen I first became interested in following the alewives and writing about them, I got one facetious comment from a neighbor who said: "I hear you're writing a book about the love life of the herrin'." It turned out to be pretty close to the love life of everybody, though I hesitated at first to apply the analogy too literally. If you are just looking at a multitude of fish massing in a brook, it is hardly likely to make you think of humanity unless you have just come in from the city, or remember Times Square on the night of the Armistice. And fish, like too much else in our culture, either come under the heading of a commodity, or they are classified, being in another kingdom, as "poor fish" or *only* fish. I found out that they belonged in none of those categories. It was the inescapable, keenly anticipated hunger and power of the season, conspiring with their entry from saltwater, that made me feel so differently about them. In other words, I was drawn in. How can you start to grasp the nature of human beings and fishes without first admitting unconscious appetite?

Older instincts of pillage and greed go deeper in us than does our conscious knowledge of how to direct them. Given an opening, we usually take it without knowing exactly why, except that it was there to take. One autumn there was an unusual run of scallops in Cape Cod Bay. Nothing like it had been seen for many years. The result was a sudden drawing out of large numbers of people, as primitive in their appetite as carrion birds descending on the plains. They took out anything that could float into the bay to drag for these shellfish. They fished in frenzied haste before freezing weather might put a stop to it, and stuffed their sacks and bags to outsize proportions, often well beyond the bushel limit enforced in many towns. It was the Gold Rush all over again. Local shellfish wardens were swamped and were often not on hand to check on the catch when it came in. Towns found themselves deluged with residents they never knew existed who were applying for licenses, and many scallopers landed their catches during the night, or at landings where there was no one to check up on them.

I watched one small boat with two men in it as it chugged in to a tidal creek below a side road where they thought they were unobserved. They jumped out to push the boat onto the bank, and then both unloaded sac after sack bulging with scallops on to a truck that had been parked nearby. One of them drove the truck away while the other hopped back into the boat and soon disappeared over the water.

Just such an appetite saved the city of Seattle. While it was suffering from deep economic depression after the panic of 1897, with many predicting the city's eventual demise, a boatload of gold arrived from Alaska. A great crowd of gold seekers had begun to move through town buying up provisions, and

Seattle survived. It also got an injection of economic juices during the earthquake of 1963, when there was a renewed flow of shipments between it and Alaska; and now the city looks to the trans-Alaska pipeline for more nourishment. So cities draw, and nearly starve, and draw again, out of a human appetite that only awaits its opportunities. What aspirations may not have been founded on common greed, in all its unconscious risk?

The migration of alewives cannot be said to be as full of haphazard expedience as that. It comes in the full golden beauty of spring, when the water trickles through the salt marshes like sap in the trees, and when the tidal flats start to stir with their multitudes, and the grasses move upward toward the light of a longer day. These fish wait offshore and start to move in when conditions are right for them, a nosing in, a circling and testing that runs in with the newly born. They are forerunners of all the growth to follow, and in that context they are right on target, as balanced in their timing as the plants, and they drive ahead with a motive force and passion, strong bodies with silvery scales, who feel the whole watery world moving with them.

After the winter, the little valley of Stony Brook where the fish ran in was being gradually covered over with a tender coating of green. Sky-blue violets started to bloom on lush banks where the mosses looked as if they meant their greenness, fervent enough to capture all sight. Many herring gulls, oyster gray, cloud white, gathered near the mouth of the tidal channel where it threaded the marsh, so as to intercept the fish as they moved in. From a distance they looked like a scattering of small, white monuments. The fish gathered and coiled in the deeper parts of the channel where the water was tea dark; and further inland where it joined the brook they skittered and dashed across the shallow, sunlit stretches, where they were more exposed. Their fretted, marine-silver sides turned light blue, pink, and gray, with a sheen of golden brown caught from the stream bed, since they are able to change pigments in response to their surroundings.

As they hesitated, darted ahead, and circled on their way upstream, their great round eyes seemed to drive ahead of their own adventure. It was an heroic procession, more so than I first realized. "But", I was told, "they always do the same thing." Well, I am not sure the same couldn't be said of any of us who are unable to shift beyond the accepted routine we might confuse with living. The stature of this major migration left repetition way behind. It was a response to the rhythm of the seas and their play with earth. The tribes were on the move. This was an annual event that rivaled the rising of the flowers, the explosion of leaves. These circling messengers from the living sea showed us the kind of ceremonies we ought to be attending to. In each of their anonymous, ten-to-twelve-inch bodies was a fire that surpassed finality. I had thought for a long time that the alewives, unlike West Coast salmon, did not, with some exceptions, die during their freshwater migration. Later I found that this was true only for a relatively short run, such as this one, which amounted to less than a half mile from saltwater to the headwaters where they laid their eggs. The shorter the inland migration, the less stress on their systems. Even here the journey took a great deal out of them. They do not eat on the way up, and they grow gaunt and weary. When you see them falling back downstream after spawning, they are covered with fungus growths as a result of their stay in freshwater, and they are obviously spent. Lengthen the journey and the mortality rises. The farther they go, subject, among other factors, to higher temperatures than their systems are accustomed to in a marine environment, the more energy they have to expend, and are in an emaciated condition by the time they spawn. At Love Lake in Maine, where the alewives have to make a twelve-to-fifteen-mile trip from the sea, there is a 90 percent mortality among them. When you know the cost, you respect the largeness of the enterprise.

I stood on a wooden bridge that spanned the brook where it ran through banks covered with reeds, cattails, and poison ivy, and watched the forefront of a small school of them swinging their way upcurrent, flashing in the light. Suddenly approaching the bridge, they turned back. When I moved off it, I understood why. It was I, the strange, animal shape, who had stopped them. When the obscure, wavy mass, as seen through water, was out of the way, they darted upstream again.

At the head of the valley, where they have to climb a series of fish ladders just below an outlet leading from the ponds where they deposit eggs and milt along the shallow edges, in a whirling, thrashing dance together, the concrete pools were packed with them. Down in the pools there was a crowd of children and a few adults standing waist deep with all their clothes on in the cold, running water. The panicked, trapped alewives leaped violently as many hands tried to hold on to their slippery sides. When the children caught fish they threw them up in the air, shouting and screaming, wildly looking at each other for approval. Life in ignorance seizes its foreign counterpart. "Grab 'em!" "Throw 'em to me!" "Mine! Mine! Mine!" they cried, along with the gulls making their own excited music down a bend in the brook.

Now and then, a thoughtful individual, shocked at the undeviating character of the mass of fish, shocked at those that kept trying to leap a rocky falls to the side of the main stream, to be injured or killed in the attempt, would ask: "Why? Why do they do it?" It is hard to face the implacable terms of existence. To contemplate the life of fishes might remind you of a swimmer caught in offshore breakers, thinking he is riding them in, but finding himself, little by little, being carried out, getting weaker all the time, with an appalling feeling of helplessness at being pulled into an infinity of uncaring force. But all

the predatory people and herring gulls, yipping and screaming, certainly spared no thought about jumping in and joining
the procession. It was a ritual, verging on lawlessness, of a
season of love and death that nothing ever succeeded in avoiding. The alewives kept heading upstream and leaping the low
falls like a pulse, defying the impossible, staring ahead out of
a sea they soon returned to if they survived, leaving their seed
behind them, while the song sparrow praised the spring, with
its "sweet! sweet!" ringing out along the borders of the brook.

So we and the gulls join in unending predation. During the
migratory season, the gulls stood in wait along the banks of the
stream or on the tidal flats where its waters rippled out over
the sands to lose themselves in the bay. Having begun to look
at them as compatriots, I could sense them as being nervously
conscious of each other's rank and order. There was a kind of
uneasiness in them, as if they were half waiting their chance,
half waiting to be put down and robbed of it, and when one
gull grabbed a fish from the stream there was an immediate
rushing up and chasing after it by all the others in the vicinity.

Down the length of the stream the fish saved themselves to
some extent by moving up at night or in separated schools by
day, slipping along, delaying in deeper water, rushing across
the shallow stretches, lithe, camouflaged shadows testing their
way ahead. But there were times when there was little escape,
and I could see the gulls in their role of disciplined strategiests.

One afternoon, I went down to the shore to see thousands
of hollering gulls gathered over the flats at extreme low tide,
where silvery sheets of water only a few inches deep went trail-
ing out at the mouth of the creek, and a great number of dead
and dying fish were lying out there. flashing in the light. They
had evidently moved in at mid tide, and when it started to ebb
thousands were still pressing in through the narrow channel at
the outlet. So the gulls had them. At first the birds made low
runs over the water and then performed shallow dives with

wings outstretched as they picked up their fish. Where the stream got to be increasingly shallow they did not have much more to do than feast on top of it and peck down in. I suppose that at some point the fish were prevented from moving ahead into deeper water because the gulls kept them in a panicked state, wildly milling around, and as the tide ebbed they began to get separated and stranded all over the sands.

The alewives were lying out in the open for hundreds of yards around, their whitish silver bodies stiff and still, or flipping in shallow pools, their gills opening and shutting as they gasped their lives away. Gulls enjoy fish eggs. To get the roe, they had slit the sides of many of the herring with their beaks, but there were still a large number they had not even touched.

It looked like the carnage of battle, a mass disaster, though for the gulls it was simply a matter of convenient exploitation, and for the schooling fish a terrible but common destiny. I thought too of dead and dying bodies lying out across a city square after a revolutionary riot when the rest of the crowd has finished battling the police and fled away, down the long streets and the side alleys. Sublime energy, the great hunger, leaves the participants in its history behind. While the survivors moved on, I imagined myself left behind, lying out trembling and wounded, then thrashing and hitching off to try to reach deeper water and safety.

Hours later, great numbers of dead fish were still lying all over the sands, many now picked down to bits of ragged white flesh sticking to slender bones. "Looks like a dump," I heard someone say. Garbage across the flats. Exploitation proceeded across an open planet, unexplored, unfinished in us all. At this level, gulls and men shared the same simple motives, though the gulls might be more in control of their native limitations, swinging with the cycles of plenty and starvation, because as experienced opportunists, it was their style, whereas we seemed to back in through ignorance of our own excess.

CHAPTER 6

The Ancient Mystery
of the Fishes

Fish are an unknown, from another realm of experience, but I learned to see them as my friends. We moved in orbits far distant from one other, but we also found our way as best we could as members of a vast fraternal society that filled the sea and land. They brought me out of myself, showed me the great measures they had to obey, and sent me on the run along with them. That they were beyond me and came from outside me only held me to them.

Fish explore most of the major and minor currents of the globe. They ride outside our vision in the surf. They loaf and scavenge on the floor of the continental shelf, and explore the great rivers. They eat with spontaneous ferocity, and like salmon on their upstream journey, plunging giddily out of the water, many seem to be on the verge of flight. They never stop circling and nosing ahead, as the sea birds also circle and scan the surface waters, journeying with deliberate, inevitable daring.

They have mastered the universe of water that covers the major part of the planet. I have met only a few of their twenty thousand species, but each of these has illuminated the place I found them in. They pout, wiggle, and dart. They hang in glassy eyes of water, or in a downstream current. We see them, in their scaly reflections of water and sunlight, shining past our capacity to see. There are silver-sided minnows sailing straight over the brilliant sands; marsh killifish making quick dashes across the bottom of salt-marsh ditches, to disappear in puffs of mud; and in the seas beyond, the mackerel with rippled patterns on their beautiful fusiform bodies, slipping and flashing through the waters.

I used to fish for big-mouthed black bass in New Hampshire. Their stiff, spiny fins were like large thorns. Their white flesh, veined with fine black traceries, made the best possible food, and when I smell their slick freshness in my memory, I smell the lake waters they came from. Their green suspension in the lake was part of its own sleep and waking as it held its counsel for thousands of years under ice or summer lightning, with an ebony shine that reflected open nights of stars. I also watched orange-bellied sunfish calmly waving their fins over shallow depressions where they laid their eggs, with a kind of time-honored dignity. What better initiation could I have had in the proprieties of the earth? Then there were the alewives, later on, with further instructions in the joined communities of life, a major race bringing in a packed sea message every year, leading ahead, a congregation of muscles, sensitive nerve endings, pure sight, blood, eggs, and sperm, a great fortune to be risked and spent.

On their outward migration, the alewives keep moving down toward saltwater out of the ponds where they spawn, letting the water take them in places where the current is strong, circling and hesitating in the lower reaches of the salt marshes, finally moving back into the bay and beyond over the continental shelf. The bay is only about eighty feet at its deepest, and begins to drop off from shallow waters near the shore at about two and a half miles. On its bottom is a marine wilderness world that most people never see unless they are on board a trawler, though tokens, like skate-egg cases, dead spider crabs, sand dollars, and other organisms often land on the beaches, particularly after storms. During a collecting expedition with a group of high-school students on board, the crew lowered a net from the stern of the boat and then hauled it in by a winch, to unload such a mass of frantically moving, slippery life all over the deck that the girls all screamed at once. Stiff-tailed skates with a rough skin that looked like the light stubble of a beard, and with mother-of-pearl bellies, were curving, swelling, and subsiding in their agony. There were little sculpins with winglike fins and ragged backs camouflaged for algae-covered rocks; there were small sand dabs with speckled skins, as well as other varieties of flat fish in shades of brown, pebbled with red or black, along with red crabs, spider crabs with studded, snouted carapaces, and big, reddish sand dollars.

The haul was thrown into a tank full of water, examined and identified, and then returned to where it came from; it was like a sample, for those of us who had become accustomed to a reduced environment, of an original, unexpected largeness. At the same time, all this strange, violently flipping, crawling, heaving life came from a first place we sensed in ourselves, from a presentness in nature rolling forward out of the past. Everything here belonged within a vast framework of earth history, an unending hunger. Whales should be ploughing the waters in great numbers, dolphins dashing after fish, windrows of bait fish breaking the surface where they were chased and panicked by feeding fish beneath them; gannets should be diving from their heights and sea ducks gathering and departing. In many areas they still were, an abiding example of the scale by which all things are measured. In the house of our mother the sea there are many mansions.

The fishes range from tiny slivers, splinters of light, to a powerful size, like the striped bass with smooth, lucent colors gained from the sides of the sea. When thousands of stripers mass through the water, twisting and turning, as John Cole wrote in his book *Striper*, the sea bottom is sometimes churned up and a dingy "sand rile" obscures the surface. Along with the weakfish and the blues, "the primary schooling, toothed, muscular feeders of the inshore territory," they are "the mass killers of the silverside, the mullet, the herring, the shrimp, the tinker mackerel, the blueback and the bunker. When a school of three hundred or four hundred stripers receives its simultaneous feeding message from impulses not yet fully deciphered by humankind, the creatures detonate a group frenzy that shatters the water's surface with the violence of an erupting undersea geyser."

Nothing more than the head of one of these big predators fished out of its element can put you in mind of a savage and original world you can only approach with a sense of awe. I remember the head of a big bluefish a fishermen had left behind. It was a cold, water-smooth blue-gray, and had a great yellow eye with a black iris. It lay there in its dead pride like a broken monument, and was being fed upon by a red crab.

One cool, spring evening on the outer beach, a number of fishermen, at intervals of several hundred feet, were casting into the surf and then sticking their tail rods into the sand, waiting for a strike. Nothing happened for well over an hour. Then a number of terns which had been flying back and forth as individuals along the shoreline started to flock together and to dive into the surface for schools of small fish. It was then that the action began. Our of failing light, in out of sea mist that screened the horizon and enclosed the long beach so that it

looked like a stage, one big bluefish after another started to
smack into the bait that hung out in the surf, to be hauled in
and lie heavily thrashing on the sand. Because of the fishes'
teeth, which can cause ugly wounds, the fishermen extracted
their hooks with pliers. The bodies of the fish, heavy, smooth,
and dark in the evening light, looked like bold officials, captured from another world.

That other realm, of course, full of intermittent frenzy and
voracity, is ours too. No matter how much we try to temper
it, the urgency will not stay hidden. Fish are in the unseen
horizons behind us. They come in out of them to say that the
old world is in pursuit of the new.

Fish court each other, protect territories, migrate, and reproduce their kind with varying degrees of devotion and intensity.
Rivals and aggressors too, they arouse rivalry and aggression
in predators like ourselves—wars have been started over herring—and some envy. What people most like to repeat is that
big fish eat little fish. It is an image of grand devouring with
which we are familiar. Fish have innate responses common to
other animals, and they also have unique ways of their own.
They use fins to gesture with. They possess sense organs that
respond to light and temperature, as well as disturbances in
the water, and are used for orientation in any given body of
water as well as for the perception of other fish close by. They
are also capable of learning, especially with respect to changes
of place. As many fishermen know, some fish are very good at
learning how to avoid a hook. But fishes are still an enigma, and
what we know about their learning abilities is still in its infancy.

One day toward the end of April, instead of jumping the
salt-marsh ditches as I usually did on the way to the beach, I
sat down beside one, and there I watched a procession of fun-
dulus minnows, otherwise known as mummichogs, or killifish,
some striped, others smooth, blunt-nosed, stout-bodied, both
large and small, parading in the sunlight. Their motion was

fairly slow and deliberate, though individuals would make wiggling dashes across the sandy bottom, for the purpose, I since have learned, of dislodging ecto-parasites from their skins, and when I moved they all fled madly toward the far end of the ditch. So I watched them for a long time, drawn by their common motion to the point that, like an astronomer with his head in the stars, I thought: "Take me with you." In fact, many of the male minnows, whose bellies would later change to a buttercup yellow color in mating season, had backs spotted here and there with white and yellow, like specks of sand illuminated by the sun. Then, in the middle of this sedate parade, passion swam in.

I suddenly became aware of a small fish, not more than about an inch and a half long, which was slanted, head down, toward the bottom, rapidly waving its fins. Its belly was a cardinal red, and with the sunlight on them its eyes appeared to be sky blue. I guessed it was a male stickleback, building a nest, and, from the size and color, the four-spined variety, or "bloody stickleback," which spends its life in the marshes. He was constructing a small mound, with a hole in the center, and would move off, spew out sand, and return as he shaped it. When the nest was completed, the stickleback would gather the eggs laid somewhere in the vicinity by the female, who was not to be seen, and deposit them in the nest cavity. Then he would guard them during incubation.

While he was at work, head down, fins fanning, the whole body vibrating like a kite in a fast wind or a hovering kestrel, the minnows flitted idly by and he would dash at them, one by one, and they would leave that precious space alone. Some were much larger than he was, but it did not concern him. Then another stickleback left the nest he was building about four or five feet away and intruded on the nesting ground of the first one. I have never seen such a show of instant warning. Each one a glowing red, with open mouths like fire pits, they whirled around each other several times and then separated, the intruder returning to his own nest. They also flashed thorny ventral fins that shone a bright yellow like a knife unsheathed in the sun. It was a swirling, cape-displaying dance, the unleashing of beautiful action in the cause of temper and protective feeling. No harm done, and they returned to business. Lying down on the still partly dormant marsh grasses on a cool New England day, I realized that I was present at one of the true pagan rites of the world.

Later in the season, it was to be the turn of the male minnows to start displaying. But now they moved calmly back and forth in the shallow water, while the nest defenders made quick sallies in their direction. Both shared the salt-marsh cosmos. Minnows protected sticklebacks, in the sense that the ceremony of association puts tolerance and pugnacity together in the same weave. It was "something understood," as the English poet Henry Vaughan put it in a great poem about Christian aspiration. I in turn had been pulled in to the rounds of a fire dance that defended all of life, not excluding our own. The little fish held me to profound arrangements. Below that I could not name what held us both.

From the perspective of human intelligence, as science knows, comparisons with other forms of life are often misleading, but the earth's repeated ceremonies, whatever enacts them, never excluded us for lack of the right interpretation.

During one summer spent in Maine, I heard shouts coming from the inlet below the house. It was in the evening, and I had been watching flamingo-colored plumes flinging across brimming walls in the sky with haphazard abandon. There was a small reversing falls there which was used to run a sawmill in the eighteenth century. I would judge that the tide, coming in across Broad Cove from the open ocean beyond the islands, would have been strong enough to run such a mill up to sixteen hours out of every twenty-four. The water was now flowing out strongly from the millpond behind the narrows, now simply a natural basin joining an estuary that winds back into some confined salt-marsh areas backed by a bowl of hill country covered by fir and pine.

I found that the voices came from a boy and a girl in their early teens who were jumping around in high excitement because of some fish they were trying to catch by hand. They had grabbed two, which they had thrown out onto the seaweed that scarfed the rocky, muddy shore, and there the fish, menhaden, bunkers, or pogies, flipped and thrashed, sending up whips of spray in their expiring frenzy. The girl started over in their direction, saying: "You two keep quiet!" The nature of dying seems indistinct in fishes, not something we pay much attention to, but they seem to have disturbed her, all the same, arousing some protective feelings in her.

Their purpose, they told me, was to get some bait, so that their father could go fishing. I lent them a net, with which they hacked away for a while, beating at the water, yelling and jumping around, and they managed to get a few more. Then they quit, since it was starting to grow dark. The tide was running out now, full force. There was still enough light to see some of the fish going out with it. Gray things, hooded with a silence, fast as deer, they went, one by one, two by two, with an occasional audible rush down the low falls. Then they veered off into wider waters, heading out in the direction of the setting sun, toward that part of the sky where Pisces would swim near the great constellation of Andromeda, a million light-years away.

Like those quicksilver alewives that stormed Stony Brook each spring, menhaden were members of the great family of herring, protected by their own numbers and at the same time victims of them, preyed upon by whales, cod, haddock, tuna, bluefish, gulls, gannets, and men. Over the continental shelf, the pogies travel by the thousands, or hundreds of thousands, but they are not often seen so close to shore. Perhaps the recent

arrival of bluefish in Maine's coastal waters was responsible for
driving them in, the bluefish being lusty butchers that chop
wantonly through schools of menhaden, leaving a great waste
of flesh, blood, and mangled bodies behind. The pogy is an
odd-looking fish, with a scaleless head that takes up a large part
of its body. It lacks teeth, since it is a vegetarian, feeding on
plankton by means of gill rakers. It has a dark blue back and
the silver sides of the alewives and sea herring, but with a brassy
luster, and is twelve to fifteen inches long.

So much for the mild plant eater, a food of the hungry sea;
but when I first saw those few fish running by me in the evening light it was their vehemence that surprised me. They
plunged. Their motion was characteristic of a multitude that
has to spend much of its existence escaping from hunters. They
belonged to aboriginal America, with the buffalo, the passen-
ger pigeon, and the caribou, all great, plunging herds. They
seemed heroically wild to one whose crowd had tried to neu-
tralize all wildness, and even a little mad in a violence of motion
that ran away from all mortality.

The next morning, the clouds over the water spread smoky
gray fingers across the sky, and then a long spinal column
started to form upwards, a stem curled like a pipe cleaner,
made by a jet airliner. The clouds dispersed to some extent
and the sun came out. A few of the fish were still there thrashing in the inlet, where the tidal current poured out into the
cove. The mad menhaden moved up into the flow, circled back,
then swung to the side. I thought that I ought to learn my day,
my hours, and my minutes from them, since their timing
seemed to lead me out in a far more compelling way than any
instruments available to me. This was not a poor fish, nor even,
in a particularly useful sense, a cold fish. The school in its
wheeling and roaming was one of the world's essential populations, and in their vehemence they did more than escape,
though escape seemed to shine from their eyes.

A big white and black osprey flew in over the millpond,

hovered for a minute with cloaked wings, circled lower, rose again, and suddenly plunged, coming up with a menhaden in its talons. Then the fish hawk flew off toward a huge nest piled on top of a dead spruce further down the shore, moving overland, possibly to avoid the black-backed gulls that sometimes flew up and made it drop its food. From a distance, the fish it carried looked like a solid carving, or a heavy medallion made of some whitish, silver material.

The smell of fish again off cloudy waters . . . I don't know their names. I only attend the feast. Fish are still a mystery to me, even when I sense my attachment to their tribal rounds, or when I see them caught out, like herring in a net, slashing the air with silver light. What subliminal miracle created them? They are on the other side of my mirror on life. The symbol for Christ was a fish, oval-shaped like the almond that signified virginity in religious art. He it was who fed five thousand people on two fish. And the initial letters of the names and titles of Jesus in Greek, namely Jesus Christ, Son of God, Savior, together spell the Greek word for fish. So the fish was a password for the exchange of food and light, an unknown that came into being to bind us together, like the silver minnow offered by a male tern to his prospective mate in order to cement their relationship. "I give you this sacred food to make you mine."

CHAPTER 7

Gulls and History

I never stayed with the herring as a subject, any more than they waited for me, though I suppose I could easily have spent the rest of my life worrying about whether I had got the story right. During the course of my hesitant approaches, in any case, the surrounding world began to turn out to be an expanding neighborhood, in which I was encouraged to move on. After all, life was too short for me to stop. The herring gulls and the great black-backed gulls, which attacked the alewives during their migration and widely scavenged for the rest of the year, were certainly among the most immediate, unavoidable members of that neighborhood. I never learned enough about them to satisfy me, but I constantly met them and knew enough to recognize a hungry associate on this planet when I saw one.

In reality, coastal dwellers have not been able to keep away from the gulls during this century simply because their population has gone up commensurately with our own. They have been able to exploit the exploiters. Early in the twentieth century the herring gulls numbered a comparatively few pair, breeding mostly in the northern parts of the Atlantic shore. At last count there were 700,000 or more along the eastern seaboard. They are not universally welcomed, though it may be that part of the reason for their abundance is that we have tolerated them, along with the city pigeons and the English sparrows. They plaster roofs with their lime. They are an occasional menace on airfield landing strips. They abuse their welcome at holiday picnics on the shore by stealing your food. They also steal scallops from men who say they have the first claim. In addition, they make serious inroads on nesting colonies of terns, their graceful, smaller cousins, principally through occupying their territories or moving so close, during the breeding season, that the terns can't tolerate them.

The gull population was able to increase to such an extent because of the waste food made available to it as a result of advancing cities and the activities of multinational, offshore fishing fleets. Gulls are wide-ranging scavengers as well as predators, but in the centuries before the white man showed up their numbers were held down by limitations in nature. Fledgling gulls had to shift for themselves after the parents stopped feeding them, and often died during their first winter, but with new food supplies available to them at many different parts of their range, they began to survive and the population expanded.

Watching the gulls at the town dump, as they stalk and quarrel over what edible refuse they can find—and the range of choice is astonishing, from chewing-gum wrappers to bits of tinfoil which happen to have rotting food attached to them— you might gain the impression that this was primarily an opportunist, an animal that might otherwise have very little on its mind. It appears to be a belligerent loafer, though with a latent and sometimes uncanny ability to organize in pursuit of its prey. With our help this bird may have been infected with a city and suburban spirit, a crowded, competitive type in constant conflict with its neighbors, trying to get the upper hand. In other words, they have caught a little modernity from us, being, on the other hand, unable to write or to manufacture automobiles; but they retain an enigmatic independence, and move to the wilder shore when they need to, exploiting further ranges as they have always done.

There is a pale yellow light in those expressionless eyes that has endured the terms of a soul-defining, soul-destroying sea for a very long time. They cry out in voices that run the tonal scale, shivery, raucous, often lilting and like a bell, a music with the accents of the rocking waters, and their supple, muscular wingbeats remind you of the motions of marine fish. To see a herring gull's wing in cross section is to see the outline of a wave. It is a perfect plane, made for graceful idling, for bending and beating in the air with masterly ease, for using its force or giving way to it. A gull's tail is cupped or fluted when soaring and gliding, and when the bird stops and turns, the tail spreads out into the shape of a scallop shell. They flap slowly over the water; they make long, easy glides down to the surface, and lift again; they hover on the wind or wheel idly and pleasurably on thermals high in the air.

All my life, I had listened to their shivery screams, their "uh-uh-uh" as they traveled by, and had taken them for granted. They had cruised over ports of call wherever I went, but I began to see that they were part of an inheritance I barely understood. They were a reminder of the way things were and the way they could go on being, with or without us. Now that they lived with me on closer terms, I heard deeper calls of alarm, excitement, and greed—ancient of days. If no human beings existed it would be as close a statement of cosmic belonging as any. The gulls looked out on the world with indifference to much that was outside their own interests, and so far as their survival was concerned, this seemed to have worked to their advantage, at least for the time being. Not that time mattered very much. The gulls might suggest to us that we were not so worthy of attention in being new—only a million years or so on the premises. We were, in fact, notoriously inexperienced when faced with the logic of those old maxims "Waste not, want not," and "Haste makes waste." While we advanced in the direction of more confusion because we were unable to dispose of the wastes we created, the gulls at least were not able to pile any more mountains on to the supply.

Their eating capacity, however, is something to behold. I have seen them swallow an eleven-inch alewife down whole, straining and gulping, and then follow it in a little while with another. There used to be fish weirs off the Brewster flats which had netting strung on long poles, gracefully curved festoons that reminded me of the coifed caps of nuns. The tides would leave them decorated with clumps of eelgrass and seaweed; and horses and carts, or in my day, an old pickup truck, used to be driven out to collect the fish they trapped. The gulls got inside these enclosures at mid to low tide and gorged themselves on the fish that were twitching and flipping on the sands. I walked out there myself one day, and some of them were so loaded that they could hardly flap their way out of the nets to get away from me.

I had some help from the ethologists in getting closer to the gulls. I learned that when a gull stretched out its neck and raised its raucous voice to the sky, or engaged in "grass pulling," a displacement activity to relieve tension, it was communicating in a manner that was not unlike what my human neighbors were doing. These "thieves and murderers," as Niko Tinbergen called them, were also, as he pointed out, part of disciplined communities, especially during the nesting season, when individuals were not foraging just for themselves. Gulls on New England shores start courting, or show such tendencies, weeks before the waves of songbirds come in during late April and May. As the direction of the wind was increasingly from the south, there always seemed to be a pair of great black-backs standing together beyond the beach, their handsome black-and-white plumage contrasting with green water and white sandbars in the distance. The male mght be working over a small flounder, while the female stood by and watched, with a semidetached, semisuppliant look. The fish's brown back was dotted with black, and its fins showed a salmon pink in the sunlight when he lifted it up. It seems likely that the pair was mated the year before, because they displayed with a kind of wedded ease and pride. One bent its head and neck slightly in response to the other, which bowed low and grandly to the ground.

To begin to know the gulls better is to visit them on their colonial breeding grounds, where they have no competitors and show all the basic behavior of animals organized to assure their own future. One early June my wife and I and two friends set off from the island of Nantucket in a Boston whaler to visit the smaller island of Muskeget, where the gulls were nesting, having routed previous generations of terns and laughing gulls. I have had gloomy feelings on Nantucket, feelings that began many years ago when we were stranded there for several days by a cold March fog. Ghosts of harder ages lingered in my head. It is a lovely island, and it is also out on an uncompromising ocean where shelter in our sense of the word means very little. The sparse life and brutal discipline on some of the old sailing voyages must have put a sailor on nearly the same survival level as a gull. On one vessel, seven men were put in irons "for stealing a cheese." Nantucket used to be a town that took its widows' walks personally.

There was the whaler *Essex*, out of Nantucket fifteen months, with twenty men aboard, sunk by a whale in November of 1820, 2,000 miles west of the Galapagos. Some of the few who returned after weeks in an open boat suffering in "spissy darkness" or under an "inquisitional sun," as Charles Philbrick put it down in his poem "A Travail Past," had "survived off themselves"—human flesh hung in strips and dried in the sun.

Being out on the water on that fiberglass pancake of a boat was no real hardship to us, but the waters veered around us on their eternal wandering. The cool, gray air was full of damp, oceanic smells. The green Atlantic encompassed us with its constantly choppy, running seas, and the shallow water over which the boat went spanking away was full of crosscurrents. On our way back we had to look out for shoals. These inter-island reaches could be dangerously deceiving, and boatmen could not entirely depend on channels that shifted from one part of the bottom to another or just disappeared. No one could predict, from one year to the next, where they might be.

Muskeget is a sparsely vegetated, sandy island, an outer frontier, with a small marsh in the center, where we found a marsh hawk's nest, with four white eggs, lying in wet ground surrounded by a thick growth of poison ivy. Down the narrow beach at the water's edge two herring gulls were pecking and tugging away at the great head of a striped bass, still attached to the spinal cord, from which a fisherman had cut away the meat. Other gulls, herring and blackback, were nesting in the beach grasses behind the shore, and they flew up yawping or hoarsely baying as we walked toward them. Their travel between the nests had resulted in sandy, beaten-down tracks, radiating outward, avenues of approach used many times. We watched one herring gull fly off after robbing a neighbor's nest, left unguarded a little too long. Half an eggshell was in its beak, with the yolk dripping down as it flew by. This inspired a story about some men who were out on a drunk one night, somewhere on Nantucket, and were compelled to steal three cars, one after the other. Since they could not drive them very far or get them off the island, they abandoned them on side roads or in the dunes and threw the keys away.

"Such people should not be allowed in this world," one of us remarked. "It might be that this is the reason gulls have managed so well to live along with people. They are very much like us."

We came upon a half-grown oaf of a blackback chick, where it was hiding in the shelter of a few weather-beaten boards, keeping its head out of harm's way; then another, newly hatched, with its down not yet dry, next to an egg with a beak waggling through a hole it had made in the shell. If they stray too far from the protection of their parents' nesting territory, young gulls are often attacked by adult males, who strike fiercely at them, clamping on to their heads and yanking away, and they are lucky to escape alive.

You suppose that this savagery is one way to maintain order and prevent a dangerous transgression of bounds in a limited area, but that gulls are like us may be hard to admit. There seems to be no humor among them, none of the saving grace of pity or conscious tolerance. Tense males, because of their profound attachment to a few yards of nesting territory, threaten each other, standing ground or giving way a little, trotting stiff-legged. There is a profound seriousness in the whole tribe, a sort of Puritanical attention to duty, spared of all luxuries but greed, all pleasure but sailing in the air. It is a people mutually on guard: "I am with you. I am afraid of you." There we may begin to see analogies, if not before.

A Sunday trip to the dump, now given the more pious name of "sanitary landfill," or walks on the shore, can give you glimpses of the gulls' world, but the breeding grounds are where you see the community at home, full of bold, interacting feelings and expression. These birds were making their primal music long before we settled in. Theirs is a sustained life of protectiveness and murder held in check; it is an armed camp in the interests of the future of its race. The gull society faces danger from the center of its being.

If you watch them long enough you begin to notice that some gulls are more dominating than others, some more authoritative, if only by the response they get when ringing out the alarm. You begin to see what the behaviorists found in them: the hostility of dominant birds toward transgressions; their threat displays; their ambivalent feelings toward each other; the degrees of intensity they show between friendliness and aggressiveness. Terms like these are derived from our own emotions, despite our distance from the psychic world of birds, and gull watching is likely to bring out some ambivalent feelings in ourselves. I have met people who had been made very uneasy by them, perhaps because of a displacement of intensity in their own feelings, the sense of emotions roughly parallel to their own concentrated in absolute terms in an entirely different context. The utter boldness, the lack of compromise, is not easy to face; and it can be an odd feeling to see "non-human life" with emotional relationships that are as urgent and vital by earth's standards as your own.

This may be dark living we do not want. At the same time, this semi-isolated gull domain, cold, raw, and unenviable, is familiar enough somewhere inside us, as if we were back in some grim, medieval time, trumpets on the walls, alertness by day and night, a crying of alarm in the dark, a scalding sense of life's shortness in us, and an elementary rivalry for life's essential food in our hungry spirits.

All populations, including the human animal, may be displaced by others in the long run, a process we pretend to think we can circumvent or manage with logic and the mind; but the most compelling of all logics is that of life's defenders in their mutual law as faced by outer circumstances. The protective community, out of long-tested rules, guards against eternal risk and danger, seas and skies of unrelenting power; it is in balance with the trials of infinite space.

A sense of the uncompromising hunger in all things went with us as we left the island, setting forth over the old world of the sea, which held the boat in only temporary security as it bumped away over the waves. Approaching the shoals, we began to move cautiously over the cold and dangerous waters.

Time and time again, I went down to the shore for exercise in an open world. The winds raced over wave crests in the distance, a perpetual victory with which I could never keep up. The outgoing waters of Paine's Creek shivered and swirled, racing by sandy corners. The light of the sky was the universal king. Glassy-backed beach grasses skitterishly waved on their hummocks in low dunes. When a big south wind moved in after a long spell of cold weather, it blustered about its arrival in town. The omnivorous herring gulls and the blackbacks traveled on velvety wings, and their screams grated. The wind flailed the beach. Farther out on sandy floors at low tide, fourteen crows were pecking away, flying up and down like black cloths in the air, a midnight-lichen black. The grueling surf pulled back to deeper water, while the shore kept running with its anciently vanishing and recurring music. They and the gulls were in charge of all history. The population of stones on the lower part of the beach was a true revelation. They were covered by sand one day, uncovered by wind and water the next. Round, ready, and pure in their exposure, they occupied the round world, the sand grains tearing past them, all buried and born, born and buried. This had been our day, our daily bread, since the world began.

PART TWO

Live with Me

CHAPTER 8

Homing

With an assurance that came out of unending exchanges with space, the alewives, the bird migrants, even the local trees that swayed and changed with the rhythms of continental weather, would ask me, as the seasonal tides went by, if I had learned where I was, and I had to answer: "Not yet." My sense of location was still at a rudimentary stage, and I might have lost all confidence in improving it if I had not decided, after another restless period, that it was better to stay put then to run off. The twentieth-century traveler does not soon come home to roost.

Certainly, if I had paid too much attention to what the economy said about the land I moved to, I would not have stayed there very long in any case. First, it was only an abandoned woodlot, full of scrub trees, and worth only twenty-five dollars an acre at best, and years later when the real-estate market and the developers began to take hold it had turned into a potentially profitable investment, which might have kept my family secure somewhere else for the rest of their lives. Either way, it had a cash exchange value that never indicated it was worth living in for its own sake, or even tell me where it was except on a map which ignored the landmarks. Maps, it occurred to me, could not be read by the real pathfinders in this region. That alewives should migrate from some unknown distance at sea to a narrow waterway like Stony Brook was one of its best possible identifications. I wondered if any of us cared about it to the extent that they did. And if a pitch pine found Cape Cod to its liking, or a white pine was such an ancient believer in New Hampshire that its progeny sprang up in the myriads as soon as we had abandoned an old pasture, then we ought to be consulting them about home territory. We had moved to a country that was constantly rediscovered and claimed by beings with universal guidelines. The one thing they could never do was devalue the place they lived in or returned to. That would surely mean the obliteration of their lives and their directional knowledge.

In a world that tells you where is everywhere, it is no simple matter to get your bearings. Although I still had a few human neighbors who were sticking it out and seemed to know the points of the compass, I was not at all sure that they would be able to hang on long enough to supply the rest of us with guidance, and as it turned out, they hardly managed. Yet the fish and songbirds came in from great distances, the mayflower found the appropriate place by old paths and abandoned wagon tracks to spread its leaves and hug the ground, and the sharp, pointed beach grass held down the dunes with flexibility and pride, making windblown compasses on the sand.

That same science which could send a camera off to take pictures of Mars, and, later, Saturn, millions of miles away, also told me that a mere beach flea was capable of performing some amazing feats in its own right. There is a little pearly-white creature that lives on the beaches feeding off piles of rotting seaweed, and its name is *Talorchestia megalophthalma*, for its white, protruding eyes. This beach hopper has to live in a humid environment, because though it lives out of water it still has gills. So it feeds at night, to avoid drying out, and burrows in the sand of the upper beach during the day, a hole it abandons to dig another the following night. The eyes are apparently used to ascertain the altitude of the sun, the place of polarization of light in the sky, and the position of the moon. This creature, with its odd, sideways hop, can leap fifty times its own length, which seems to make it a champion among animals. All of which is scarcely an achievement of mind, but it is of such embodied genius that the earth's progress is measured. I could not help being impressed by whatever oriented that little animal, whose house was a temporary hole in the sand, to reference points far beyond its immediate horizon.

You have to suppose, with or without much knowledge, that we don't attach ourselves to a place merely to get away from another one. While human culture seems to be acquiring the role of a substitute for nature, I suspect we also learn from whatever reaches are left inside us to match the earth's, and whatever of its sensual messages we innately receive. Otherwise, why should we roll in the first snow, or rejoice all over again at being visited by the fragile, white blossoms of the shad blow in early spring? Have we not experienced them before?

The first week my wife and I moved in to our newly built house a flock of geese greeted us by flying past the window during a snowstorm, and for some years deer would step out in the late afternoon to browse in a field not fifty yards from the door. In the growing springtime the tender oak leaves hung before us in all their light and shimmering curtains of pink and silvery greens, and I knew scarcely the first thing about their ecology. In fact, when I first started reading about that new discipline, the idea that each life was so aptly fitted to its environment was a little difficult for me. Influenced by a world flung out in all directions, I must have had the notion that anything might be anywhere. Still, I sensed that we were in the right place when we finally moved in, like those alewife fingerlings that head out to saltwater from the outlet of the ponds they were hatched in. They have never seen the sea before, but its image is in them.

I could now watch the passing weather touch and define the place I lived in. I could reassure myself that we had built at a centrifugal point, which migrants from hundreds or thousands of miles away flew in and identified. I could begin to see that the common forms around me, such as the countless blades of grass, the geometrically distributed leaves on a tree, the barnacles flicking out their feathery feet down by the shore, were displaying the great co-equality of life. They acted as receivers of the sun and of global currents in the waters and the atmosphere, each a reflection of surpassing complexity. Every life that touches on another, or becomes part of another, keeps the earth's fluidity in being.

To locate ourselves, we needed to be located. If the warblers failed to arrive in May, how would we recognize our station between the continents? When we left home we could quickly join the highways and airlines of the world. They had succeeded, along with all forms of modern communication, in making a good deal of local, which is to say connected, travel unnecessary. Despite the telephone, which crossed many voids, there were areas between us and our neighbors, near or far, which we no longer needed to explore, because they were so easily and quickly passed. This also amounted to a loss of local hospitality, in terms of people who could help you on your way and give you directions.

Yet those "compulsive" birds and fish, like the ever moving and changing clouds, kept homing in, roaming and circling, to turn the land and its waters into a center for universal travel. I had to inquire why it was that many of these other forms of life still knew their way across the surface of the globe through such an amazing variety of sensate abilities, while we who were supposed, by all accounts, to share in life's multicellular, neurophysiological connections, and were long-distance flyers into the bargain, seemed to be losing that innate sense of where the earth's great headings were. It would seem that the intellect that probed these matters was in need of more companions.

A phoebe showed up from South America, wagging its tail, pretty much on time by comparison with the year before, and seemed to say, in its dry little voice: "Here am I, ready to nest in your eaves. Let me stay." And I felt that any fool would who knew how much we stood in need of directions from such a reliable partner.

As time went on, I learned to recognize the terns and plovers, the yellowlegs, the sandpipers and songbirds, when they came in off the flyways and sea-lanes of the continent during the spring, while the wintering eiders and brant geese flew away to northern breeding grounds. Some passed through, while others stayed, taking part in a dynamic employment of the ranges of land and sea. Many shore dwellers knew tidal time as intimately as we know night and day, and they knew sidereal and sun time and could find their way accordingly. The long-distance migrants could take advantage of landmarks, ocean currents, and the wind, and they were able to use information about the earth's magnetic field. They carried earth's directions in them, ancestrally, genetically. Young sooty terns fledged in the Dry Tortugas off the southern tip of Florida migrated in their first autumn all the way across the South Atlantic to the Gulf of Guinea in Africa, which they had never seen before. Nor did they have the benefit of adult leadership, since the adults left their breeding grounds after nesting but appeared to go no farther than the Gulf of Mexico. The young did not fly directly. The route they took was apparently 20 percent longer than that which could be traced on a direct line across the Atlantic, and it was the most favorable one, facing them with less resistance from prevailing winds.

This inherited sense of direction plus the native ability to fly great distances was not a random business but was tied in with the fact that populations had to be homogenous but dispersed at the same time, consistent with the breadth of the ocean and the periodic nature of its food supply. Still, it seemed astonishing and exciting that a young bird, only a few months old, could take off across the Atlantic without any prior knowledge of where to go, a kind of ancestral daring in nature to which we were only half-awake. Was it right to call them limited because their journeys were only unconsciously motivated? To say that human beings needed consciousness to survive while birds did not seemed to put their use of the unconscious on a more accomplished level than ours in some respects, or to make us more wholly conscious than we seemed to be.

The green turtle could find its way from the coast of Brazil to tiny Ascension Island in the middle of the Atlantic, 1,200 miles away, where they nested. Said Archie Carr in his book *So Excellent a Fishe,*: ". . . it really seems impossible that turtles or terns could ever gather at Ascension—and yet they do." Take into account the theory of celestial navigation as it might apply to turtles, or of inertial-sense dead reckoning, or piloting with landmarks unknown to us, or response to the Coriolis force, and then logically knock each of them out, as he did, and you were left with the irreducible fact that either all these factors were involved or that there was some sense in them that we knew nothing about. The great mystery in terns or turtles was their inner synchronization with the changing conditions and ranges of the planet. That may be why some of us, still circling, backtracking, confused by our own directives, might be envious of them.

What did these consistent periods of arrival mean, as I began to note them down in the local phoebes and swallows? Nothing fixed, in a particularly useful sense. (We like it that way, but may be the poorer for it. Besides, the swallows of Capistrano were late last year.) Migrations usually came in waves, and those that were "on time" might be only the vanguard of more to follow. They might be pioneers who were more adept at arriving when expected because they had done it before, which certainly seemed true of the alewives. Many migrants were lost along the way. Many were thrown off course by storms, or moved in the wrong direction by contrary winds, or, if they were fish, by ocean currents. Migration implies searching, or even hundreds of miles of drifting, for some marine species, as much as a fixed and conscious directional movement from one place to another, though some migrants, particularly birds, could be amazingly sure and direct.

Some of this I learned through observation, and more still through natural history and popular science. But it was not only the coordination of these animals with earth's conditions that lifted me beyond the facts, but also their often mysterious affinity with its elemental reaches, like an arctic tern traveling up to twenty thousand miles a year between the Arctic and the Antarctic, a bird that experienced more daylight than any other creature on earth; it was a bird of light, engaged in an ancestral practice that challenged the planet.

On a whole-earth scale, the timing of these migrations was headed for timelessness. I had been too long confined to dates. (Would I never swing off the undeniable security of the calendar?) Days, on the other hand, days in space, days under the sun, days and nights, shadow and light, forever passing over us, trying out, were the measure an unemployed migrant might be looking for. The need to seek and be centered was as vast as geologic time. And all factors came together on some day in early spring when I heard the high, sharp whistles of a yellowlegs along the shore, announcing its arrival from the southern hemisphere. What could a poor calendar do in the face of that? The bird came in and set me free again.

In part because I was none to practiced in finding my way, easily lost one morning only a few hundred yards offshore when the fog suddenly rolled in, and none too sure of my bearings when I strayed too far from the asphalt, I knew we had much to learn from these explorers, since explore they did. If they were "simple," then so was I. You could doubt, even if we eventually discovered the precise mechanism through which birds found their way, whether we would be able to exploit it, as one account suggested, for our own purposes. By the time we got to the point that we needed some computerized device borrowed from pigeons to tell us how to get to the home loft, it might be too late anyway. Our brains would have lost connection with our legs.

It could be said that we were turning into perpetual migrants with no recognizable place to go to, continually exchanging houses and land, so that Cape Cod could be the same flat, insulated place we were trying to make of Arizona. All life explores its environment, but we seemed to be doing it to a fare-thee-well. I suspected that we needed to return to places we had long since forgotten, such as those the fishes knew.

In response to inner command, not only baby fish or sea turtles but also human beings might still have a sense of the way to head when faced with unknown waters, but we had lost faith in it. Perhaps we were only neglecting directions we felt we no longer needed. Still there was a residue of old seas in us. It stemmed from an ancient part of our natures that we were a little afraid and turned a little wild when watching hordes of fish move inland, or saw the unfolding of a leaf as a new event, off at the edges of experience, or felt the diving of a young seabird from its breeding cliffs for the first time as uncanny in its depth. Nothing was yet found.

I stood on a cliff above the open sea and felt that there was something of me running through its currents and its eddies. I watched continual explosions and disappearances taking place in those rolling waters threaded by sunlight, where unseen legions of fish were roaming, muscularly vibrating under the surface. At times, from a boat offshore I had seen long wind-rows of foam where bait fish were being chased to the surface, firing the waters with their motion.

It was over the offshore waters too that the white gannets with their six-foot wingspread wheeled from high in the air and then pitched in, sending up jets of spray. Those strikes, those recognitions, went on all around me, and though I had traveled far and wide myself I had hardly begun to recognize them; but they come back, if we are on hand to receive them, repeating their directives for our benefit.

There was, for example, the reappearance of my turtle. As a boy, with the wish in me to capture, I kept a painted turtle in a pen, and it surprised me by laying eggs, thus revealing a secret identity. The eggs were eaten by some marauder, though I had desperately wanted to see them hatch out, and later on the turtle died of unknown causes. I suspect it had something to do with mismanaged captivity. I gave it a formal burial under a big sugar maple that stood over a rock wall. I also carved my initials and the date on the plastron, or undershell, of another one. I can still feel the black, low, shiny-smooth, hemispheric shell, like a water-worn stone, and the little black legs with clawed feet that felt as soft as the pads on a puppy. Red-orange, yellow, and black are first colors for me. Then, many, many years later, with all kinds of human displacements and holo-causts in between, I met it again as it ambled slowly across the grass out in front of that same tree where I had buried its com-patriot. And I thanked the turtle as an old friend, not only for the pleasure of meeting it again, but for bringing me back into one of those mutual, lasting circles never stopped by the passage of time. It was like another lease, smelling of apple blossoms in the spring, the way they were and would always be.

Though I had a late start in learning my directions from the life around me, the lesson of the turtles was reassuring. They were educators who knew how to take their time. Someone once carved their Cape Cod initials on the shell of a brown and black and yellow box turtle I met while it was peering up and moving slowly ahead through fallen leaves, and so I found it to be twenty years short of the century mark.

That box turtles did not travel more than a few hundred yards or a quarter of a mile from their home territory did not mean that they lacked a deep sense of location. When displaced, which happened when the ignorant and innocent took them away from their native areas to city apartments, they were completely disoriented. So I was grateful that we had box turtles around us, with their scraggy yellow necks and the reassuringly antediluvian look in their little eyes, to help place us, or, for that matter, advise us to be satisfied with where we found ourselves.

We needed one kind of turtle to tell us how to cross time in one place, as well as another who was an expert in crossing the seas. This homing business ought not to be wholly entrusted to human beings with nothing more than mechanisms to deal with it. It ought to be left to the professionals, such as turtles, frogs, toads, and salamanders, as well as birds who, in the art of wings, could come and go over thousands of miles. A study of California newts by Victor Twitty—*Of Scientists and Salamanders*—showed that when displaced from their home creek they returned to it, through forests and gullies and over a mountain ridge a thousand feet high. This was their breeding stream. On the other hand, since some of the males captured along the way showed no signs at all of sexual development associated with impending breeding activity, it seems that their ability to home in in such an impressive way had more to do with the right place to live than the right place to breed.

Toads have returned to breed in ponds that have been destroyed by road building. All landmarks were wiped out, and still they possessed their wonderful sense of where home was, or ought to be, in a featureless new landscape.

The homing instincts in these creatures of slow travel was invisible to us, and we did not seem to get close enough with the kind of biological tampering that suppressed their hearing, their sight, or sense of smell. Could we not ask the same kind of investigative question of ourselves? If we were still capable of homing in, after having strayed so far away, it might very well prove to be an attribute which was essential to our future; and we would do well to start practicing the art; though if I were sufficiently relaxed about finding my own way, or not losing it, I might not trouble myself about such things, any more than an experienced fisherman does who steers his way unerringly through fog to his home channel. If toads retained an image in their heads of where a central place was even after it had disappeared, a similar faculty could be useful to us who had erased so many landscapes at will.

We needed a whole earth and a whole sea to find out where we were and dance to its measure, either with the wonderfully swift and graceful style of a tern, or the gait of a turtle, but it should not be too hard to find if everything around us embodied it. Even the common periwinkle down by the shore could claim a kind of global conquest, taking its own good time, like a box turtle. One early spring I found innumerable black specks in the wet sand of the beach. With a hand lens, I could see the round forms of these snails, each not much larger than the wet, pearly quartz grains that surrounded them. The cohesive, rounded surfaces of these grains seemed to give the tiny creatures a temporary medium for growth, before they were large enough to separate and start their slow tracking along the edge of the tidal shore.

The edible periwinkle was not an original native of America but an immigrant like the rest of us. It evidently came over with the Norsemen in their long boats to Newfoundland many centuries ago, but did not cross the Gulf of St. Lawrence to Nova Scotia until 1850. After that it made steady progress, to New Brunswick in 1860, then Portland, Maine, where it was discovered in 1870, and New Haven, Connecticut, in 1879. It had reached the prodigal resort of Atlantic City by 1892, and finally got down to Cape May in 1928. The periwinkle is now found as far south as Chesapeake Bay. So this dark-shelled creature, with its slow roll and two black antennae pointing forward, finally rounded a vast stretch of the North Atlantic for as far as it seemed useful to go.

Symbolically the migrants are also in the stars, sliding across the waters of the sky, traveling past each other, moving on great circles the way the periwinkle did. They made up a heaven of directions for ancient civilizations, extensions of human realities. The Toltecs of Mexico wore a snail shell on their heads. The shell of a snail was an enclosure like a house that held a life inside, and also symbolized birth as the insignia of the moon god. The moon itself was connected with water in the minds of the people, and its hieroglyph was a water vessel. The Mexicans associated the moon's blue light with turquoise. It was also a prototype of growth, and of change in the weather. Even now, if you walk down to the shore and watch the shining moon reflected on the waters, that magic symbolism seems as appropriate as what can be seen through the accurate eye of a telescope. And those who finally landed on the moon to report that it was a pitted wasteland which looked like a "dirty beach" did not alter its regality.

The shell, matter enclosing spirit, was the insignia of the great god Quetzalcoatl, who disappeared in the direction of the East and the land of the dawning sun. It was said that he would one day return like the rising of the morning star in the East, where the moon, with which the star became mythically unified, had died, and would be reborn in the form of a slender crescent tilted in the sky.

The snail was identified with the winter solstice, and the slow-moving turtle with the summer solstice, at a time when the sun seems to stand still. The Mayan month Kayab, when the summer solstice occurs, showed the face of a turtle. The Mayan name for them is *ac,* or *coc ac.* The sea turtles, loggerheads, which are sometimes found stranded and frozen on our shores, and the greens, are also represented on their temple buildings, and when you look up at the constellation of Gemini you can see three stars, which they saw as having the form of a turtle.

Starry nights, moonlit nights, with the sea breathing in the distance, its tremendous gravity poised beyond us, its waves belting the shore. If I know that Cancer the crab scuttles across the tidal flats to its designated part of the sky; if I know Pisces the fish swins off light-years away, I too can follow, from one home to another. To be head-taut with the stars around you, foot secure on soil and stone, to know your direction and return through outer signs, is as new as it is ancient. We are still people of the planet, with all its original directions waiting in our being.

CHAPTER 9

The Great Weather

A land is most fully lived in to the degree that we are married to it, for better or worse, and dependent on its vitality. Yet we have acted, and this has now become a global habit, as if nature were in the van of independent human progress, and the land with it. Written large in front of each one of us is the title of that 1,200-page volume entitled Man's Role in Changing the Face of the Earth. During the great days of the trains, before the process reached its present momentum, Henry James wrote, in *The American Scene:* ". . . the country exists for the 'cars,' which overhang it like a conquering army, and not the cars for the country."

In another passage, written as if the worth of the countryside lay more in its gentle charm than in the more violent wilderness qualities which earlier and later settlers have seen in it, he wrote: "The touching appeal of nature, as I have called it therefore, the 'Do something kind for me,' is not so much a 'Live upon me and thrive by me' as Live *with* me, somehow, and let us make together what we may do for each other—something that is not merely estimable in greasy greenbacks."

We have not changed. The land is still being left behind, even by those who occupy it.

I discovered that the alewives, the gulls, and many others I met, or who met me, were hardly stay-at-homes, back-country relics. That they lived with "the environment" was clear enough, but it amounted to a dynamic occupation. They were engaged in great interchanges which went far beyond their immediate boundaries and limitations. I only wished I could say the same for myself; but they encouraged human aspiration. They were worth consulting not just because they were birds and fish of discoverable names and habits but because they turned the land and its surrounding waters into a place of great complexity and variousness that cried out for our participation. We were the ones who might ultimately be left behind. Although we thought of ourselves as the supreme identifiers, we were going to have to learn what identified us, which amounted not only to living things (not so much "things" as embodiments and practitioners of universal rarity) but also to the elements we shared, soil, light, tide, and the nearly constant wind.

In every season there are subterranean beauties and powers that speak to what lies unexplored inside us. We have unseen collaborators everywhere. At no time in the year can life avoid the majesty and precarious balances of light and weather. All seasons flow into each other, a surprise each day.

I hear a "whoom," as a full wind possesses the trees. This is both a controlled and combustible planet. Half the time I don't know what I am hearing, even when I listen. One afternoon a mild earthquake was reported, but aside from hearing a distant thundering which I thought was a plane breaking the sound barrier, I was unaware of it. I miss out on many of the great moments and crises of the changing year, although outside me there is always the long sound of running and bubbling waters bathing the earth, running down its sides.

The expected moves ahead in unexpected ways. Preceding nearly every spring, the wide bay looks like an arctic waste full of pack ice. Tables of ice are heaved, turned, and tumbled in the tides, and often locked in for weeks before warm weather draws them out and disperses them, genuflecting to each other in blue water as they die. Violent winter airs rock the trees in their iron ground, and sometimes crack them apart. Men as well as birds die in the brutal weather. Margins of safety are reduced to zero; but the doom suspended over life always gives way to it in the inextricable bonds of the year.

One dimension defines the next. We are all being sprung out by reaches we have hardly begun to explore. We may be about to experience what we have never known, because of a restless will that sweeps away our own. We are visited by the dream of resurrection again and again, no matter how blind or deaf we may be. A winter's day by the sea shares in the towering fantasies that mark all passage, say what you like about the dead cold in ourselves. The grandeurs of the weather disperse and reassemble. Through the uncertain caves of mind and heart we follow its signs.

Human society can never stop trying to control its own disorders and temper potential anarchy with some overriding purpose; it can never relax in its work of supplying initiative and direction to thousands of different enterprises. But what is that to this exalted change, in control of all its component parts, sounding its cavernous ages in the wind?

The long clouds, the thin, fibrous ones that swim in the upper light glittering like minnows, the fluffy, fulsome ones, the clouds that make the winter sky look like the eye of a boiled fish are sledded ahead and driven away. The winds drive in over seaside country from the West, the Arctic, the Gulf of Mexico. We stand in the great air, the continental trading that gave the white man his running start and his claim on "super" size, the big dream, the pioneer "conquest of nature." In a way it is the fate of Americans to live with a giant wilderness dimension which they have never really been able to hide from or to overcome. All they could do was run through it to another shore. We became addicted to size, in a sense that those who lived in "la douce France" or an English countryside would not have understood. Our special brand of spiritual darkness owes itself to a great landmass which we partly overcame, but which has never surrendered, in the sense that it never allowed the stature of its occupiers to exceed its own. Somewhere in him, an American is everything and nothing, puzzled by a space which he conquers and praises at the same time, unable to stay with the continuities, the beautiful accretions of nature, because the continent which gave him such a running start has never allowed him to stop.

Yet the wind's voice keeps repeating our location. I would miss it if it were not hissing in the trees, buffing the waters, rustling at my ear, acting savage, acting sweet. Stiff blows, sudden shifts in wind direction, capricious breezes are somewhere, everywhere. Wind drives people nearly mad at times, but it is a measure of living and carries a sure kind of timing with it, a partner in the vast synchronization of global forces that come together in any given place. At this point in my life, I have to respond so as to be able to testify that I am present, and not in a state of insensibility. I am not reassured by the idea of "change" running on without any identity, but changes in the wind are music to my ears. They make me listen. I rock on a sea of feeling, waiting for a fair wind. So it must be that I am listening to my neighbors at the same time. They are not moving on their own, but at the will of something unexpressed. Nature will not desert us so soon. Accidents and accidental behavior, odd fits and starts, a shifty lightning in our moods come about as we move through unaccountable flux.

So it is that a hometown often acts in strange, spasmodic ways as if reacting to unseen influences. Animosities break out and then subside. Officials refuse to resign and are hated for it. One committee fights another in public session while the chairman tries to preserve the general decorum. An emotional, elderly man dies of a heart attack at a town meeting. A hundred people go home after such a meeting, hoping never to see each other again. They all see too much of each other. And yet they know that in some mysterious as well as common fashion they will meet again, like the fish in the brook, in order to continue a journey.

The problems of society still narrow down to the terms of that precarious institution the family, with its continual need for care, for adjustment and constraint. The home kitchen is where human feelings require their rights and hide at the same time, an impossibility on the face of it, but depended on by humankind. This is the permanent state, this benign travail, this troubling need, the center where the anvils of emotion ring and the gods of growth and attrition preside over the meals; here is our salt marsh and our winter ice, where we are waiting for the spring. We were never, in any real sense, independent of our environment.

After a while, I began to realize that there was no time when some other live being did not anticipate new moods and alterations in our mutual surroundings long before I was aware of them. Birds and fish felt shifts in atmospheric pressure. Trees prepared. Their leaves "knew" when to change color and fall away. Frogs went into hibernation when I was not looking. Alewives responded to imperceptible changes in water temperatures. The herring gulls flew back and forth between land and shore with a rhythmic understanding of the tides. Animals in a tide pool, a universe which I was aware of only from the outside looking in, responded to its rhythms in terms of extraordinary sensitivities. Where was I when the light changed from one magical condition to another?

One fall day, walking through a woodland all of whose trees, gray rocks, fungi, and ferns were reacting to the season with their usual timeless patience, I spotted a light tan moth, with faint tracings on its wings, where it had alighted on the spent flower of a goldenrod. Its wings were spread. Perhaps it sensed that its time was up. Then I walked away, to come back a day later and find it again on that identical flower. There had been a frost the night before, but the moth was not dead, because when I poked it it fluttered feebly down into the leaves. They were so exactly its shade, of its own degree of faded color, that I was unable to find it again. I wondered how many frosts it would take to kill it, but in a sense it never died, and what bothered me was the way in which I could blunder in and not only interrupt this little station in evanescence but ruin my understanding of it.

Back, back in time went the race of woodland moths, fading into unending autumns and winters, leaving their seed behind them; partners, like the trees, the rocks, and the goldenrod, with an immortal patience. So life and death in the crawling, consuming, growing and decaying of the woodlands, joined the continuous rhythmic unities of the earth, carrying a million years into the present. Now they were obediently slowing down, easing up, and suspending, with a kind of divine innocence that lasted beyond human impatience. To a warmblooded mammal there was also something very cruel about this cold, slowly glittering, shadow world now moving in. This interval between a dying and a massive sleep was too uncompromising for me, who was more vulnerable than a moth. Conceding that glacial majesty, I shivered, and jumped out of the trees onto the highway, like a rabbit streaking for cover.

What living *with* began to mean to me was not so much the

gradual and quiet accumulation of links and associations between a people and their land. We had almost destroyed that experience; it was losing hold in our idiom. The local dialects were losing out. We had to recover earth and its great weather in new terms. In a machine age, we have been thinking of ourselves as self-translated, which discourages us from associating with nature on a personal basis. Modern communications say we are made of endless circuits and connecting points, all wired for sound that goes humming off into the universe. It is understood that I track myself in relation to the tracks of all others sending out their messages, and that we are all joined in the complexity of this exalted hive. But when the teeming air falls across my house, and I hear the sullen roar of the sea in the distance, I know there are other forces that have prior rights, and that as I live in their light and shadow I am no more or less complex than death or the sunrise, which are undiscovered. The weather brings me uninterpreted force and motion and meets the trial runner in myself.

The way the atmosphere behaves in January is no more "normal," or predictable, in spite of its recurring patterns, than it was in August, or will be in April. When do we lack similar, unpredictable disturbance and turmoil in our own experience? We are still part of the forces of the sky, and its potential victims. The earth speaks in voices that are distinct in us, and at the same time continually changing. The sky is flying, not toward a neatly assembled collection of cumulus clouds, but toward infinite combinations.

CHAPTER 10

Chroniclers of the Year

*A*ll you have to do is settle in with what much of the human world calls nuisances, such as earwigs, moths, moles in a lawn threatened by weeds, mice in the walls, and squirrels in the bird feeder, to realize that your place is not entirely your own, that, in fact, you are occupying someone else's place. All the guns, poisons, and herbicides at our command are not going to be able to eradicate all prior inhabitants and make our human house any more sacrosanct, safe, and civilized than it has any legitimate right to be. I cannot forever keep out the wood-pecker that mistakes my house for a dead tree. For that matter, why should I object to a flicker banging away on the roof when what it is doing is proclaiming the triumph of spring? I own no feast drum which can do it half so well. One year a gray squirrel gnawed a large hole in the back wall of the house when I was not looking and managed to raise a family in the attic.

By the time I became aware of it, there were three teenage squirrels up there that I was able to grab by the tail, since they were not yet wary enough of human beings, and throw them back out the hole. War, if you have to have it, but let us not assume that all these other spheres of influence can be isolated from our own without our implicitly choosing a vacuum.

When we dismiss any "wildlife," plants as well as animals, as useless to us, or insignificant, we risk doing the same to the whole passage of the earth around the sun. These lives not only accompany spring, summer, autumn, and winter. They miraculously join and define them. Without them, what would we have with which to compare and justify our own occupation of the year?

For many years I passed by the flowers I met on the way with only the dimmest understanding of their graduated role, from early starflowers to late asters, as interpreters of light. Although I am still ignorant, with much catching up to do, I finally arrived at a day when I decided to stop, in order to begin to see. I had noticed that the California poppies I had planted from seed in our garden were regularly opening and closing every morning and late afternoon. So I sat down next to a whitish flower around four o'clock in the afternoon, when many of the others had already contracted. Minutes passed before I noticed much difference in that dish of petals spread out to take the light. Then I saw that it was definitely beginning to change. The motion was there, though nearly imperceptible, and the flower had begun to deepen and narrow into a cup. The stamens and pistils began to disappear at the base, the petals were closing in, settling, adjusting themselves like the interfolded pages of a rolled newspaper. It was about three-quarters of an hour before the process was completed. Finally I was aware, after nearly a lifetime of neglect, of a whole new cosmos, though barely glimpsed, a whole new dimension in time and space, even a new way to measure our existence.

Wonder of wonders! For a while, I was unable to cut a flower without worrying whether or not I had severed it from its appropriate universe.

In early spring, the days slip by gathering in clarity, but I am never quite sure what is going to happen next. The light is magical, falling like a golden oil across the trunks of the trees. It is strange in the mind. The life of light, felt before me in watery veins and currents, held in the tissues of the plants, known through cellular shifts in the soil and in the bodies of the trees, comes to a relative outsider. At least, I have not been educated in it. I feel an off-centeredness in my surroundings, and I do not know where it takes me. I certainly do not act in terms of all those facts and exactitudes I was brought up to take for granted. A confusion of dreams is what I know of the well of certainty. Each genuine creation is arrived at obliquely. We can never look the sun straight in the eye. But in the midst of this misty promise, the starflowers are born, as clear a creation as anything could be.

They and the wood anemones, which grow with them on the woodland floor, flower for only a short time, so I have to take care not to miss them. They are both slender and thin-leaved, with delicate white blossoms that stand out conspicuously before much else has bloomed and attract early bees and bee flies, going through their complete cycle before the leaf canopy of the trees shades them over. The wood anemones are perhaps better described by their other common name, windflower, both because they are wind pollinated and because they look as if they were made for shivering and shaking in fragile elegance as the spring gusts blow across the ground.

The pointed leaves on the starflowers, placed on an umbrellalike whorl on their stems, have the texture of finest paper, and they are very delicately veined, with a slight wrinkling to them—a flutter at the temples—the skin of still water under a breeze.

These early flowers, with their delicate sexuality, reserving a first place in which to make sure of their future, make an unqualified offering of themselves. They are as perfect in their identity, as exceptional, as the warblers that fly in a little later on, to make bright stitches in the May cloth.

In June I learned to wait for the whorled loosestrife, flowering in open patches at the edge of the woods. Each of its four-, sometimes five-petaled flowers is delicately projected on a stemlike thin wire from a whorl of five lance-shaped leaves, and they are star shaped, orange-yellow, with a circle of red specks at the center. These leaf circles climb the stalk of the plant, level after level, and the whole looks like some little Chinese pavilion or music box decorated with birds and flowers, meant, with all its lightly built, perfect appendages, to tinkle on its gentle rounds and bring in other sympathetic harmonies. It is the appropriateness of these plants, and hundreds more, within the wheel of the seasons, that gives them a magic power of their own.

On clear spring nights, the stars of the Milky Way run foaming and glittering, but pitched as delicately as the loosestrife, reaching out, level after level, responding in expanding space, as the sea breathes steadily beyond the shore. There is no end to the exploration and use of space by the children of light.

Originally, at least after first sight, we learn about birds and flowers through books, identifications, and categories, though a great many species, especially those inhabiting the earth's rain forests, are not yet known to science. We have left mythical naming behind us, as well as the oral naming that comes through necessity and long acquaintance. Perhaps as a result, even the most familiar birds, and doubtless the flowers too, keep their enigmatic and elusive character, like those bright warblers that seem to appear out of nowhere in the spring. They are exceptionalists, flitting and twittering through the shadow of the trees, quickly seeking, restless little dynamos, in shades of yellow, black, pale blue, plum, and orange-red; and they have the quality of being able to turn the landscape into something more than it was. They materialize as things of the spirit, coming to the right place at the right time, so as to identify it themselves, out of deeper sources than human reason is able to command. All things are born again through ice and fire.

"Where does he spring from, the deer, the deer, the deer?" goes a chant from the Chippewa. Where indeed? I heard a girl of Sioux extraction chanting a poem about a water bug: "the little water bug" that skims and circles on the surface with such quick delight, and she interspersed her words with that ritualistic "way-hayway" of the Indians, a sighing, deep as wind and water, a reaching from the lungs to embrace and receive. Where does the little water bug come from that helps us meet the out-running circles of the earth? Why assume that the final answers will ever be available to us? They are unwritten.

Coming in or going out—the deer, the deer, the deer; man, woman, or child—we are at best or worst alone; and there is unending talk of the social and material means to combat it. At the same time, the nature of this gift of arrival and departure is inclusion, beyond the moment in which we live. To share is to see for the first time. To belong is to listen to a song you have never heard before. In the earth's marriage bond, in the simplest act, are millions of years of transformation. Nature, multifarious and secret, has no end of new beginnings and overleaps at heart.

It is the encouragement of openings that counts for more and more in a rigid and divided world. I used to help lead natural-history field trips for children during weekends, or after school hours, when some of us were trying to start a natural-history museum. It was elementary education in a form that was close enough to the elements to suit me. I did not feel that I was teaching them so much as joining up. We recruited our students for a month or two at a time, led them toward salt marshes, bogs, ponds, and pitch-pine barrens, explored the beaches and the tidal flats, and then saw them go. It was a wonderful experience in first acquaintance, even for those who had spent their lifetime in some professional capacity. Being able to bring a child into closer association with a tree, a frog, or a moon snail was a success in itself. You feel yourself, with all your relative ignorance, becoming a mediator between unformed youth and the tides of creation. Or that was the frame of mind it put me in. I learned from the sharing. It was like attending to the various phases of the fish migration, as I walked along the banks of the brook; we seized, with hand and eye, on new attachments, along the way of a great process we had only started to follow.

Such temporary classes might seem somewhat removed from the state of family life, when the children are permanently your own, but the same process is there to follow, in a deeper association. It is an often difficult, dismaying education for parents, which some individuals might very well not choose if they could review what was coming up. But it is the woe and joy of reality, in the pride of untamed existence, which you meet, and it is the best leader. You enter into deeper and more subtly precarious realms that you were aware of, over which the only protective control you have is love, though this is great enough. You encounter states that are strange and withdrawn, spontaneously open and merry, sweet and generous, uncompromisingly sick, continually following the only original language, that of unconscious nature, which we try in vain to analyze. Deep and shadowy are the waters of childhood. You cannot go back there and you accompany them half in apprehension, half in delight, watching a process that is now a little removed from you, growing on its own like the clouds, taking unpredictable form. But without that company we are deprived of the deepest examples of everything in untaught experience that guides the greater life we belong to, in the stature of its becoming.

So the world of life, having been so terribly put apart from humanity, toward its increasing impoverishment and our own, gives never ending evidence of its potentiality to move from one state of awareness, affinity, and sensate wisdom to another. It is our true guide. We originated there. And when we watch the perennial practice of fish, birds, mammals, and plants adjusting to the places they have found right for them, adding to their dimension, we can mark it off as another corroboration of the true nature of where we live. In our lasting domesticity are wild directions.

Green cattails speared up through the mud on an edge of the marsh. The call of redwings floated over, while frogs made their watery, subway sounds—"rrumm-rrumm"—under the sky of May. I caught sight of a yellow warbler overhead, and then another. They were mating on the branch of an oak tree. The exquisite little female suddenly turned herself into a bow, head and beak tilted on one end, tail on the other, and the male quickly copulated with her. They made a little burst of solar energy together. It was all over in a second, their daintiness and ardor perfectly matched.

The yellow warbler, handful of light, *Dendroica petechia*, common in willow thickets, shrubbery, and orchards, breeding as far north as Alaska and Labrador, wintering from across the southern tier of states down into Central and South America, as far as Guyana, Brazil, and Peru, a transcontinental treasure. I heard the song of the male tripping from its throat, a quick, definite series of notes, very pretty to hear, with a lift at the end of the phrase. While his mate was plucking fine, silky strands out of the catkins of a willow which grew at the water's edge along with wild rose, azalea, and inkberry, he fluttered up and down chasing insects, a neat little skipper along the tree limbs. I watched him catch them between the tender new leaves of the oak, which hung in their delicate shades like limp but ready hands in an obedience to the sun. After a while, he joined her, and I saw them dive down with beakfuls of silk to the place they had chosen for their nest, the crotch of a tall inkberry bush.

The nest was securely wedged between the branches and the shiny leaves, molded by the body of the bird in a process that took three to four days. The final result was a firm cup, between three to four inches across, woven delicately with grasses and willow silk, with a few fibrous strands of bark around it, like hoops on a tiny barrel. Such graceful and tempered work to go into the making of a home! Why should anyone need a five-room house to be born in so as to brood over one's existence?

Eleven days after I first saw them mating, there were five tiny eggs in the nest, a very light, subtle gray in color, with brown speckles. As I stepped back to watch the nest through my field glasses, a big snake, a black racer of the kind you often find in these watery regions, slipped quickly over the ground. I heard a "tsip" from the female warbler, and saw wild alarm in her eyes. The snake's noncommittal eye slanted along the side of its head, like all the malevolent portrayals the human race has made of it, but it only slithered off and disappeared into the marsh.

A day later, and the eggs were gone. Perhaps the snake was the villain, if it managed to climb the shrubbery, or a red squirrel, or a blue jay; and it worried me that I might have come too close and brought attention to the nest. At times it seems as if the whole natural earth fought its own provisions for the future, but in the long run the care is as preeminent as the loss.

So I saw, through these precious, recurring signals of the year, that we too were provided for, and that the elevated role we claimed for ourselves was an illusion.

CHAPTER 11

Living with Trees

The seasons turn. Hang on. We are off for another ride. The tide rises higher with the full moon that presides over the flats and imitates daylight between the trees. Spawning fish and sea worms, insects and plants, must be responding to it in any number of magical ways. I myself walk out into the night and feel someone else in me talking to a light beyond him not measured by human control. It is a matter of new dimensions out of old phenomena, a tugging at a half-initiated spirit. However angered and enslaved by circumstances we may feel, the life in us is not allowed to quit. There are changes and reassociations going on in the soil and in the atmosphere, revolutions of a more reliable kind that move us to feelings we never knew we had. To have real rather than sentimental roots is to be in motion.

That will introduce my ignorance of trees, which grow out

of life's original sources on terms I do not fully understand. In spite of that, they have been my lifelong companions. I have climbed them and built houses in them. I once built a house-boat of white pine to explore our lake, and it meant a wonderful freedom to me. I have cut them down, and even hugged them, as a boy, in moods of loneliness or affection. They hang on from a past no theory can recover. They will survive us. The air makes their music. Otherwise they live in savage silence, though mites and nematodes and spiders teem at their roots, and though the energy with which they feed on the sun and are able to draw water sometimes hundreds of feet up their trunks and into their twigs and branches calls for a deafening volume of sound. Their major endurance is good to count on, and how would we know a thing about the art of longevity if we cut them all down? If trees have analogies to human families, and I am sure they do, how can we clear-cut all their relatives, young and old, not to mention ancestors and descendants, the stock of generations, and expect them to accompany us as useful resources?

Trees identify their ground in ways that ought to be highly advantageous to people who are beginning to lose the sense of where they are. The fact that much of New England has become heavily forested, since the decline of intimate agriculture and the family farm, has inspired talk of a wasted resource. One would think it was a resource that had come back to tell us what kind of a place we live in.

In how many ways, in green and white New Hampshire, did those great hemlocks, white pines, sugar maples, and shining birch not grasp me by the arms and seize my heart so as to give me bearings! How could I have learned to walk without them? Those wonderful trees, a great architecture of living on, their geometric graces in balance with all the extremes of the year! The hemlocks' long, outward-reaching, feathery branches rose and fell in the wind, lithe and limber in their open swinging, sometimes shaken into cranelike dances, while the tall white pines would shudder with their loads of silvery needles glimmering in the sunlight.

Trees are open to the asault of a vast number of insects. All you need to do is examine the leaves of a deciduous tree in midsummer to realize it. Flying insects, crawling insects, chewing and sucking insects, leaf miners, leaf hoppers, borers, mites, myrids, innumerable larvae, never let them alone from their tender emergence until the season when they sense the change in light, stop manufacturing food, and fall off. The respiring, perspiring, food-fixing trees, with their great numbers of leaves all arranged so as to receive as much radiation as possible, have attained a major equilibrium between the uses many other forms of life make of them and their own putting out to feed on the sun. Their structure is also a major statement against adversity, standing in the center of extreme heat and cold, various degrees of freezing and thawing, the chance of lightning, heavy loads of snow, ice storms, and violent winds.

The woods we moved to on this sandy peninsula are primarily composed of oak, including white, black, post, and scrub, with an understory of witch hazel, blueberry, huckleberry, sheep laurel, and viburnum, plus, of course, the pitch pine. Because pitch pines are "intolerant," or greedy for light, they will die when overtopped by other trees. The result is that they are losing out where the oaks have been allowed to grow. Not too many individual pitch pines get a chance to grow to great height, except in sheltered hollows by themselves, and even there the wind sometimes comes roaring in from the open shores at sixty to seventy miles an hour and may crack a big one in two. Sea wind and salt spray tend to keep them down, even for several miles inland, and the oaks, which have been incessantly cut over for centuries, have been weakened by insect borers, fungus, and rot. They do not make the best-quality wood, but as stove wood, or for a fireplace, they burn slowly and well. To split oak logs, especially when the wood fiber snaps in freezing weather, is a pleasure to me; and the cut wood smells good, though "piss oak" is an old term for the black oak.

Their gray trunks are spotted and plated with lichens, some a pale, seashell pink, some gray-blue, others a light green. As you look through them, it is as if they were only a landward extension of the marine world, different forms of the same space. Water, too, is the life of lichens that require a share of mist and dew, of fog and rain. An abundance of fungi and lichens on the trees indicates a wood that has been neither burned nor consistently pruned. In terms of management, it implies lack of care. Since I have not cut down the trees in a very selective way, cleared out the understory, or burned all the dead wood, my neglect has opened up these acres to the greater standards of the wild.

Fungi, which may grow on dead or dying oaks in the form of pink or orange clusters, curling or cuplike, are often hard to tell apart from the lichens. They are plant life which preys on either living or decaying matter, whereas the lichens are agriculturists, cultivating small algae within themselves, protecting them, in return for a share of the food they produce. They are, in fact, made up of an alga and a fungus. These two species join in a single partnership so precise as to produce a lichen that can be scientifically determined as a distinct plant, but both reproduce separately. They have to discover each other, through spores borne widely by the wind and water, so as to produce a lichen of an identifiable species; although friable reindeer moss, which is a lichen, can regenerate from broken fragments if the ground suits them. Lichens take their own slow time about growing, and one you spot on a rock may be centuries old. Apparently, the partnership is not always secure, because, in isolated instances, the alga may be parasitized and killed off by the fungus.

The lichens are delicately beautiful, with colors that complement the bark of the trees. Some are branching, corallike; others have crenellated edges like a flower or a cloud; still others have dotted, wrinkled, or tufted surfaces; and some branch or fork out like flames, or seem to be on the verge of spreading forward like waves. Although they are an original form of life with provisions for an indefinite future, they are unable to tolerate industrial smoke, or air that has been polluted by chemical wastes and gases. They are the signs of a cleaner world.

Lichens belong to an endless suspension in time out of which lives sense their moments of affinity, their opportunities to parasitize, to bond or devour. It is an awesome game, hanging on eternities. The existence of a lichen depends on the centrifugal nature of all contrary forces, on a scale that seems perilous to our short-term sense of things, though exhilarating in the mind. We are just insecure enough to wipe out these primary plants. On the other hand, isn't the human personality itself made up of seemingly irreconcilable components? I wonder how *we* hold together.

So the society of trees—with their companions in a fire of blue light—move on while standing still, tested as they grow by all the combining, convening forces of earth and atmosphere. They are sinewy and tough, erect in their vicissitudes, and their own version of desire, taking their symbionts and predators with them. They do not give in too easily to their destroyers. Cut the oaks down ten times over, and unless you bulldoze out their roots or destroy the ground beyond repair they will sprout up and take up even more space. It is as if they said: "Extermination is not our destiny."

Older religions had no trouble connecting men and trees. A tree was the tree of life, magical bearer of fruit, container of mercurial speech, a trunk with a god inside. At times, when one of them was injured or appeared to wither, a man's life might depend on the outcome. In Europe, certain trees were supposed to have healing properties. Denmark still has oaks that are centuries old. When I was there I was told that a few had reached a thousand years. They had been spared because they grew on the king's land, originally set aside as hunting preserves. An old farmer named Jacobsen, who had some interest in the life of birds, told me that he once rode his horse into an ancient, hollow tree and was able to turn around inside. I was shown a medium-sized oak with a gap in the middle through which children were passed so as to ward off what he called "English sickness," characterized by bad teeth and weak legs—no great compliment to the English.

Old belief may seem weak and childlike to skeptical minds that judge things on the basis of objective verification, but it saw the roots of things. It knew trees, as it sensed itself gone to earth in the process of growth, decline, and death.

In my search for an education in correspondence I owe a great deal to names. *Quercus alba* almost satisfies me in the sight of a white oak, and I could busy myself for years on end with the principles by which a leaf or a needle is adapted to the wind, the leaves of a popular twisting on flattened stems, the thin needles of a white pine hanging and swaying in silvery compliance with every air that reaches it. Yet the trees are always asking more of me. I know that their staying power needs further exploration, more than one civilization to solve it.

I listen to the wind swishing through the pitch pines and seething or rustling in the oaks, while blue jays bounce cockily overhead, conversing in brassy, insinuating tones. I sense thousands of years between their voices, hanging millennias. Time opens out again, as the trees hold up their pinwheels of needles and their lacy twigs in the carousel of the wind.

Under the full moon, the ground is a network of intricate shadows, meticulously drawn. The trees seem to move across the fluidity of light, extending electric arms and fingers. Their trunks are braced against the wobbling, racing planet. They seem to lift me with them in a sailing of their own. We go between yesterday's wind and rain, today's jubilant, far-reaching light, the revivals of the weather. Another sunset comes to fill the sky with molten colors like tropical birds, crossed by golden, braided strands, an impermanent wall for sight, while next to my bare, encrusted flesh, the bark and trunk with which I meet the air, I am with trees. We wait, and we move out at the same time. It is not only the long distance migrants who make daring leaps into the unknown.

CHAPTER 12

Commitment

When any of us move into a new community, we act in a way that is roughly parallel to that of some of our fellow mammals. We inspect the premises. We gather our belongings together and put some family mark on the wall—an etching, or a photograph. We move tentatively in the direction of such neighbors as it seems safe to approach. We inquire about where to find the goods and conveniences we want. Then we gradually discover who is sympathetic and might ask us out, or who might be asked in, feeling toward appropriate circles, in other words, a little nervous about possible hostility and by the same token eager to be accepted. Finally we sense who the safe ones are, and find out where the bank, the post office, and the grocery store are located, and so send the children off to school. In testing our boundaries we are as much affected by an inner weather responding to an outer one as any chickadee, or one of those little whiskered muskrats with shiny brown coats that I glimpsed occasionally when I am walking across the salt marsh.

In an unjustly neglected book, *Of Men and Marshes,* Paul Errington wrote: "About the edges of the crowded territories what a muskrat does is conditioned by what its neighbors permit. Even when acquaintances permit close approach, or when there is some common sharing of marsh tracts or habitations, stranger sooner or later meets stranger if a muskrat ventures past its neighbor's territories." So there is irritability, friction, and quarreling among the muskrats. In the Dakota and northern Minnesota marshes where he studied and trapped them, they meet extreme limits during the winter months and often have to endure appalling hardships. A particularly severe winter may kill off large numbers of them. Their remaining food may be frozen in the ice. They are often forced from their lodges to wander desperately in search of food, and fall victims to minks, dogs, foxes, and cars on the highway. They may freeze to death or die of wounds they get from fighting each other, and cannibalism under these circumstances is not unknown. But for them, as with all other species, the ruthless side of nature coexists with its moderating and life-giving qualities, and muskrats on the whole seem to be moderate creatures. "They are unimaginative, practical . . . meeting slowly developing problems by default or by improvisation forced by patent crises."

Since I am neither a trapper nor a game manager, like Paul Errington, my acquaintance with muskrats is fairly distant, but I suspect they must have a benign life in our coastal marshes as compared with Minnesota, though the ice locks them in here as well, especially toward the end of winter. There may be nothing enviable in the life of a muskrat. At the same time, it is perfectly clear that we are just as utilitarian as they are, and even more combative, preoccupied with possession and trespass at the same time; and though the answer to our problems must be moderation and humility, how many are sure of those qualities in themselves, in this overcrowded world?

To encounter the conditions of the year, the dead-end winters or ice-melting springs, in ourselves, is the best ground from which to sympathize with our "fellow creatures." Nature, in any event, was never one to tolerate mere lip service. Commitment is the truth, and reality of life and death, the whirlwind, and the sanity of light. The black-capped chickadees, so welcome because of their busy cheer, are just as seriously involved as the muskrats. They spend the year bouncing around our house as if to remind us that they are closer through clothes, culture, and constitution to the wind and weather than we are. At the same time, they are wary and respectful of the weather in its rougher moods. Their feathers are soft and long enough to insulate them against freezing temperatures, up to a point, but driving sleet, ice storms, or wet snow may kill them, and they do their best to keep dry. At night they choose the leeward side of trees and thickets, and often seek out sheltered places like holes, tree crotches, or even abandoned nests to roost in. They are not only very small birds but sensible ones. Other, similar, wintering birds, like the tufted titmouse and the tiny, nervously active kinglet, know how to find snug shelters too, though I have never seen a kinglet roosting at night. It is hard enough to spot them during the day.

One March afternoon, where there was a perceptible change in fronts, with a north wind laden with cold moisture just starting to move in from the open shore, I noticed a flock of chickadees starting to congregate in a group of pitch pines, like so many people moving into shelter out of a storm. (They certainly feel bad weather, in whatever it is in them that corresponds to our bones.) A little later, I heard much crying and twittering in the pines and looked up to see a pair of tufted titmice, crests raised, their beady black eyes, so I imagined, being full of a wild excitement, just as they flew away through the tops of the trees. Evidently the chickadees, which had been making grating, clicking-and-clacking cries, were upset by this intrusion into their chosen shelter. After all seven of them had routed the titmice they rested quietly, each light gray breast showing against gray mists, wet needles, and the scaly, dark trunks of the pines. Wind and sweeping rain kept coming through and dying down; and I noticed, through the sound of gusts, that the little birds seemed to be conversing. They appeared to be quite satisfied now. Their notes had the quality of light grains of sand being shuffled across a sheet of paper.

Chickadees are among the most active creatures I know of. In a life defined in terms of energy this one must be in charge. They are almost constantly on the move. They are like acrobats, upside down and right side up, searching the bark of trees, every twig, each needle, for insect eggs or larvae. Their wings whir; they make short hops everywhere. Their eyesight is remarkable for picking out tiny objects, inconspicuous signs. They will dash behind house shutters or between shingles in their hunting. Their heads and bodies are continually jigging, abruptly nodding, and moving from side to side, like the head of someone with a nervous twitch.

They have an exceptionally high metabolism. If you put your ear to a chickadee caught in a banding net you can hear that its heart makes a continuous purring sound, like a tiny motor. During the breeding season they are intensely active. During the larval stages of certain species of moths, quantities of caterpillars descend from the leafing trees beginning in May, and chickadees, being early nesters, will feed on them. It has been estimated that parent birds bring their food in to their chicks once every four minutes, making something like six hundred trips a day for a single pair. So the very smallest keep the essential fires going, being responsible for many of the end results on which we feed ourselves, whether we thank them or not.

Most people, intrigued by the gaiety and friendliness of the chickadees, feel emotional sympathy for them. With practice, you can get them to feed out of your hand, or even pick a sunflower seed from your lips. They do not seem afraid. Still, that brightness in them is characteristically wild, and we do not ordinarily keep chickadees as pets. I am sure that if it worked it would be a great indignity to them. They are remarkably self-sufficient and competent as inspectors or acrobats. I suspect they are even leaders, in their fashion, since they appear at times to be in the forefront of warblers or nuthatches that occasionally travel with them from place to place as one flock.

Since I could use a little more leadership myself, I follow the birds around, listening for connections, watching them thread the daylight hours with their activities. They tell me I have hardly started. So, fast-beating heart, little anger, vehement inspector of trees, lead on; I may catch up eventually.

Their need is to spend, oblivious of time. Death is only a departure, as it is for the worker bee, who after six weeks of life, her wings in tatters and body exhausted from her complex dances and interactions with the earth, goes off on a foraging expedition and never comes back to the hive. I hear a musical hiss in the low trees, a *tzee tzee*, with a bell-like tinkle to it, a disconnected thread of sound swinging back and forth just out of reach. Then a kinglet flies into sight, pausing for a second on a branch, a teasing, tiny bird that just as quickly vanishes. What would the death of such a wisp mean at all but a disappearance into the realm of light and shadow it came from in the first place? But I have learned how deeply, savagely, a protective power reaches into the smallest of lives. Since we live just as precariously on the shores of the frost line, we too are bound to that provision which gives us life between impossible extremes.

One fall day, on one of my walks through the woods, I found the round body of a shrew in the leaves beside the road, the possible victim of an owl. It had been freshly killed and was headless, so that it looked like a tiny, lucent silver barrel, red around the rims. Now, the shrew is so short-lived and so constantly hyperactive that it makes me as a fellow mammal decidedly uneasy. One winter, during an exceptionally cold period, when they may have been overabundant, desperately hungry, and attracted to seed dropping from the bird feeder outside, the shrews began to enter the house. We could hear them scuttling and squeaking in the walls. My wife set a couple of mousetraps in the kitchen and caught one. I came in when one of the hungry tribe, no bigger than a silver dollar, was trying to drag both the trap and its dead occupant through a hole in the wall where a pipe led out from the kitchen sink. Not a rescue mission, you may be sure.

This partly blind, highly intense creature weighs less than an ounce, but has to eat the equivalent of its own weight every three hours. It will attack mice larger than itself, poisoning them with a powerful secretion from salivary glands that flow into the wounds made by its teeth. The victim's heartbeat and breathing rapidly slow, and paralysis sets in. The content of the glands has enough poison to kill a hundred mice. One bite could probably poison your hand for days. Being constantly aggravated little creatures, they will, I suspect, attack almost anything. I was once faced by a shrew that, as I walked by, slipped out of leaf cover to hold its ground, twittering angrily, and I was the one to withdraw.

Well-fed shrews can be relatively peaceful for a while, but when they are artificially confined to close quarters they may eat each other up, and will die if deprived of food for only a short time. Their normal diet seems to be composed of small organisms in leaf mold, as well as snails, worms, insects, and an occasional bit of plant life. This ravenous mite cannot live peacefully with much of anything except its mate during the breeding season. It is preyed upon by hawks and owls, as well as snakes, weasels, skunks, and wildcats. Having produced two or three families of three to ten children a season, it has done all that is shrewly possible, and dies of old age at about sixteen months.

Some Eskimo tribes believed that shrews were possessed by demons, which is not surprising, given such violence packed into so small an animal, and that they would kill people by entering their hearts. One man stood like a stone for hours when he met one, before it finally left the vicinity, and all his friends congratulated him on his escape.

Shrews being what they are, so highly-strung, pitilessly on fire, are hardly ever still, though they do sleep at intervals. They twitch, jerk, dash, and turn about, twittering as they go. Whenever I see one I am amazed all over again that anything should be able to live at such a pace, even for a short duration. I wonder if the spirit which is a shrew is not a little demonic but also holds a wild declaration of despair at its own tight destiny. Is a shrew protesting, with such almighty vigor, against what it is obliged to be?

It was a fairly cold night, around twenty-four degrees at bedtime. There was a light snow cover on the ground outside, and it contained little pits and craters, like a moonscape, where shrews and birds had been active near the feeder. All at once I caught sight of a sharp, eager little head, and a velvety gray creature with pink legs dashed over the crusty surface to grab a sunflower seed. I watched its darting, quivering movements for a while, and since I had that life history in mind, it brought such concentrated ferocity in view as to frighten me. The pit that made a shrew of me was opening up. "So that's the way you act," I thought, "when you dance the tightrope of existence, darkness before and behind." No wonder the poor animal battled with such unconscious fanaticism. Here was Scott making his way across the frozen wastes of the South Pole, doomed, but full of the fire that burns at the limits of all experience.

The balance between life and death, stubbornly ignored by

much in nature that fails to see the distinction, gaily and aggressively engaged in by a chickadee, played to the limit by a shrew, seems deeper stuff to us, only too aware of the power of annihilation. At the same time, there is no escape. Somewhere in the maelstrom of experience the shrew and I cross destinies. Length of life and the superlative efforts we put into ensuring it are not of desperate importance in the eye of the sky, no importance at all to this mite that "accepts the universe." It is incapable of trivializing anything.

During the winter, while we, on top of the ground, extend our insulation to an undreamed-of extent, the chipmunk is asleep in its underground chamber. It seems very different from the shrew, being an alert little creature, brown as the nuts it collects, diurnal in its habits, and open-eyed to everything around it. Its spasmodic, jerky movements look like another version of a shrew's, or another mode out of all the possibilities for life expression in the tribe of rodents, but the chipmunk spirit seems softer and brighter. In it the terms are lightened, in spite of the fact that both have the same lengthy list of enemies. Ferocity in one is more recognizable as fright, or alarm, in the other. The chipmunk lives years longer, sleeps, at least sporadically, throughout the winter, and seems gay and inquisitive. It is an explorer, in a different sense from the shrew, so burdened with an icy destiny. At four weeks, even before their eyes are open, the baby chipmunks begin to start investigating objects in the chambers they were born in. Their jerky, stretching, exploratory movements continue in them throughout their waking lives. They are out for more information about their environment, which is the same impulse that led us into outer space.

The chipmunks coil up in their burrows, tails lying flat over their backs, though their hibernation is not so deep that they do not occasionally wake up to feed during the winter on the seeds and nuts they have stored above ground. When they appear at the surface depends to some extent on the relative rigor of local climates. Before they disappear in late fall or early winter, they are often chasing each other with furious enthusiasm, or disappearing with a "chip!" of alarm behind rocks or trees. Tap two stones together, and a chipmunk will sometimes emerge from walls, or woodland leaves, to watch you alertly. Get up, or lift your arm, and off it dashes with a shriek. During the fall, when they are collecting food, they often sit on their haunches, twirling and twiddling acorns with their forepaws, like some jeweler in his little shop in a side street of the big city, handling a precious stone. They moisten the acorn with their saliva, bite off its sharp ends, then stow away the nut in a cheek pouch. They are intensely active during these months, constantly running back and forth with bulging cheeks, collecting food to store in their burrows. (These burrows, incidentally, can be extensive, with a number of interconnecting chambers for both food and living; and, not to be outdone by human civilization, they have toilet facilities on the lowest level.) The Latin name for the Eastern chipmunk, *Tamias*, comes from a Greek word meaning "steward," one who lays up stores.

Their constantly moving tails are indicators of their nervous state, or, to paraphrase Walt Whitman, flags of their disposition. When running, they hold their tails straight up, or stretched out. When they scold, their tails shake, and when they are seated the tails wave back and forth. Sprinting, pausing before the next sprint, dashing about with waving tails, jumping for safety under or behind each available rock, piece of wood, or fallen branch, coming out into the open again, chirping and curious, they look as newly oriented and cheerful as children. But this is a life as seriously involved as any other. When you see two chipmunks chasing each other so fast around a tree that they turn into a blur, it is not likely to be play but a dominant animal pursuing a lower-ranking one which had the temerity to approach it where it was feeding. They do not often reach the fighting stage, though even when they do they rarely get so far as to wound each other. It is a common escape-and-pursuit routine that seems to be designed to prevent spontaneous antagonisms from getting out of hand, keeping the emotions occupied and the teeth under control when they might attack family members or neighbors for no good reason.

From our point of view, chipmunks act sociably, being fairly easy to approach and observe. They often watch us as much as we watch them, and their shrieks of alarm, while real enough, sound more like exclamations than fear. But they live out their lives in a relatively solitary fashion, each to its range. Social encounter usually amounts to courtship, mating, and bringing up the young. Still, these ranges overlap, so that there are recognizable populations, and in the fall, when they are busy moving around and gathering seeds to store, they often call together. Then their "chock-chock," or "tock-tock," sounds as bright and open as the call of a robin. Ernest Thompson Seton called it "rapturous." Its real function does not seem to be known, though it is associated in the minds of some poeple with alarm calls. Rapturous alarm may make some sense, but probably not enough. I have the impression that chipmunks call that way even when no intruder is in sight, or near enough to upset them. You can hear the "tock-tock"-ing all over the side of a hill or mountain for many acres around, as they carry the chorus along, one imitating the next. It is a song that fits the season, with its special brightness of air, its falling, yellow leaves, and the openness with which another season is made ready; it also signals the coming spring, a long way ahead down avenues of torpor and cold. These may be recognition songs, and, since the chipmunk is so inextricable from the ground where it lives and dies, songs of place.

Apparently, the territory a chipmunk defends is not its hidden burrow so much as is the stump, rock, or log where it

feeds, a "food platform." That is where most of the approaching, fleeing, and chasing starts. Still, each seems to have mem-
orized to perfection the exits and entrances in its own range,
and with relation to the others around and beyond it. Their
autumn choruses ally them with a greater unity. Before the
lords of the North come down to stay, the chipmunks may
sing so as to place themselves in mutual memory. In a sense,
it is a statement about life in its holy ground. They are present,
in the greatness and responsibility of the present, while they
look to a time that surpasses them.

CHAPTER 13

The Prodigal Style

The short life of a shrew or a chipmunk, the ephemeral lives of the insects, the long life span of a human being, which tempts us to lengthen it and conquer fate, are only intervals, punctuations of an immense passage. The miseries and accidents we meet have an intensity that often fools us into thinking we have never lived. The laws of survival are harsh, and at the same time the lives that practice them are moved toward the open ends, the outcomes, spring risings in the sea. We inherit a sense from nature that regeneration never stops for mortality. Otherwise, why do none of us, in spite of everything, really think we are going to die? Immortality lies buried in our thoughts.

Cheating finality, the light flows and dances across the tablelands of the tides, where the gulls hover on the wind. The rushing, rolling, realigning waters work their way back in, and then withdraw. Under bold blue skies, or gathering and shifting clouds, the coastal waters carry and distribute their probing lives.

Flowers responding to light, barnacles flicking out their feathery appendages, fish rising to the surface, or butterflies lazily waving their wings embody the great, volatile transformations of the world around them. The hurricane is in the flower. Subtle changes in light govern a starfish or a bird. Alterations in pressure have immediate effects on the sense organs of a shrimp. The fireflies that bob along through a summer night, or those planktonic creatures that produce a similar bioluminescence in seawater, embody an extraordinary magnitude of effect. In fact, the sensitivity of living things in response to their surrounding environment is nothing short of miraculous. The secret of ultimate power that we sense in living responses and in the changing wheel of the year is what the human race has been playing with, so as to endanger the planet. We deal in nonreturnable risks. You wonder, since we can scarcely know how to disentangle the processes of our own thought, let alone solve the mysterious spontaneity of life, how we are ever to know enough so as to survive our own acts. Does the innocent warbler have more experience in the matter than we do?

Equating ourselves with living things that have such a close affinity to this prodigal and at the same time fragile and acutely sentient style is not, in Robert Frost's phrase, to institute "downward comparisons." The crucible of light, earth, and water ennobles us all, and it does not seem to matter that neither the average person nor science is able to catch up.

As William Blake put it, should there not be "senses unknown" in the living universe, trial approaches unexplored, unsuspected energies, conjunctions unheard-of, forever and ever, "trees, beasts and birds unknown: Unknown, not unperceived, spread in the infinite microscope"?

Late one winter day as it verged into early spring, I watched one of those quick-moving weather fronts that have the kind of fire in them that seems to need a special quality or state of the atmosphere to set it off. The temperature had dropped to twenty degrees the night before. During the day, the wind blew strong from the southwest, beating against the rollers coming in from the open Atlantic and breaking on the outer shore, so that their great manes plumed up and sprayed away. By late afternoon the temperature had started to plummet again and the wind blew from the north, while fast-running clouds let down showers of snow and sleet.

The bay waters to the north were violently roughed up and studded with whitecaps. Waves tumbled, rocked, and splashed along the shore. Standing at a distance, I could see their white shapes heaving just above the far rims of the salt marsh, where the gulls seemed to be flinging across the sand dunes, making low arcs in their leaping. The grasses tossed and swayed, and they carried a fire on their blades which they caught from the sunset. The sun's western reaches were of a golden salmon color, of a metallic brilliance, making a deep, pure gash in the sky. Overland the running clouds were pink as flamingos, gray as a mole. The whole sky in its freezing beauty crossed all known boundaries, leaping like the gulls from one sea to another. This was light I was unable to catch or see, integral with a motion I could only conceive of, part of the incredible speed of planetary bodies, a beauty made of an infinity of variables. But it is of such a furious unity that we, a feather, or a leaf are made, no matter how far we stray.

What any region has to have to ensure its stability are these practitioners of alliance. What are the north woods without a wolf? was the question Aldo Leopold asked. Having exterminated the wolves in the northeast, we think we are managing very well without them, but somewhere along the line eradication has its vanishing point and terrible logic, not only for the plants and animals that disappear but also for the places they inhabit and define.

What would our woodlands be without ruffed grouse? One flew into the window and broke its neck. After due deliberation, we plucked, roasted, and ate it, a consecrated host, made of sunlight and trees. The brown back of a male grouse is flecked with gold points. The wings and tail feathers are of a warm orange to reddish brown, blends of simmering light. When the bird thunders up and makes a wide circle through the trees, you can see the banded tail as a signature of gravity with respect to the leafy ground from which it just shot up. Its feathers are a great art of woodland slopes and hollows, the triangulation of trees, their shadows and fallen branches, and nothing but the woods themselves could tell you the secret of their making.

I will never forget the plumage and coloring of the arctic loon I once saw on a June trip to Hudson's Bay. Thin, cold air rode off the waters along the primaevally rocky shores while bands of clouds, the color of coal smoke, drifted slowly over the ice floes. In the light of the icy waters the stout-bodied loons that were swimming there showed a glow on their silvery heads at a distance, an electric bloom, and there were white stripes descending wavelike down their dark necks, while their broad, black backs carried white markings like veins of quartz or ivory teeth.

A feather is a global recognition point; its wearers take earth's various surfaces upon themselves. In their art you can see the perfect meeting between light and air. The glossy feather I just picked up off the ground fell from a crow, and it is pure black on the broad side of the shaft, bluish, as seen in full light, on the narrow. A blue jay's feather is iridescent, the result of a structure that reflects the light. They are intensely visible constructions for races that depend much on visibility during display or in finding each other over open distances, as gulls do.

They are also a matter of life and death, in concealment for themselves or in hiding their young.

Feathers are a supreme craft, straying off into the realm of incalculable genius. Who would think of putting those scarlet spots on the tip of a waxwing's primary feathers, or adding a halo to an arctic loon? The contour of a feather and its lightness are made for the flow and stress of the atmosphere. Its colors, sometimes drab and nondescript, often highly elegant and subtly shaded, are suited to the earth's variety.

We make blends of color, of course, and find endless uses for it, whereas birds are unable to change their uniforms. Perhaps I am more flexible and have a greater freedom of choice, up to the point, at least, where I face a traffic signal. But I share reactions to color with other animals out of an interior eye that was never self-originated. As I walk across the salt marsh again, passing through last year's dead cattail stalks and the new green shoots, a redwing not far from me suddenly spreads his shoulders and puffs out the chevron patches on its wing. The flashing red line with its white border stands out like a sunset low on the water, producing a sudden reaction in me. I throw back my own shoulders for a second in time. This is the color red, meant, like fire, to produce an unqualified response in any color-conscious creature capable of it.

Red goes deeper still. Being primitive as well as civilized, I look at the leaf surfaces next to me, seeing the red veins in a pale green leaf, then watching a tiny red mite crawling down across them, as one pulsing vein to another. One night I had a dream in which I said: "If I am part of East and West, I go down as the sun goes down." I go down, or rise, with the color red, the primordial one, fire and blood in the sky and the waters of the sea. Through that fundamental color, with all the feelings of glory or disaster it can summon up, we share with a mite or a redwing.

If the human eye sees "only" 15,000 tints out of a range that extends farther than that for some other eyes, if a fish is so much a part of its waters that it often seems to swim through them as one reflection to another, if the blue jay's feathers are only blue, lavender, and iridescent because of the way they refract the light, being in fact brown, then what we see in them are magical adaptations achieved through infinities of choice. The earth takes care of the truth in sight.

One day a fine, wild wind such as we get in spring and fall came in out of the North, with the sun shining through drifting clouds along the white and blue surf so that it blazed, primarily with an amalgam of gold and silver, but with any number of mercurial colors as well, and I thought of fish again. Where the broad reach of the thrashed waves lay directly under the rays of the sun, from my relative perspective, the light in each section like the schools that roamed under such waters all over the world, was supreme, unalloyed, impossible to adulterate, dim, or tarnish, and the mere expression of scales on a fish's body was a symbol of that brilliance in affinity which characterizes all things under the sun.

This high magic, this universal bonding, is not only in the light but in the provisions for life. What we euphemistically refer to as the balance of nature is really a continuous balancing act of surpassing scale. All phenomena are engaged in it. It uses unnumbered copepods in the ocean, seven trillion spores in a puffball of average size, billions of spores in a mushroom, four million eggs laid by a female codfish. A vast production in nature compensates for vast attrition; but in some species numbers are so delicately proportionate to their losses that they are nearly impossible to interpret. Why should a sea turtle lay an average of one hundred eggs? How did that pivotal figure sustain it in the great context of the oceans and their shores, at least before man's world came in to upset the balance? Has it been the turtle's destiny to bear in itself the right reproductive counterweight to the energies of the globe?

The sun, the wind, and the animals liberate and distribute the seeds whose mission is to plant the earth. So living things act in terms of what lies ahead of them, each race a power in the face of all the great forces that contend against it. The alewives leap, again and again, up impassable falls during their spring migration in a heroic expression of need and desire. Shorebirds and terns try again after their eggs are washed out by storms. The trees put out their intricate load of new leaves so as to take on the global measure, with a wilderness style that has hundreds of millions of years behind it. There was a time, perhaps because of the narrow terms of the world in which I was indoctrinated, when I could hardly guess I was surrounded by such extravagant statements.

Late May into June is the time of year when the pitch pines loose their pollen in clouds, so that a yellow wind passes across the landscape. It is a fact, easily found out, that this has to do with the reproduction of a pine tree, but I confess it took me a long time to look into it. So I hesitate to condemn those citizens who have been looking for a scapegoat for this phenomenon. There is a suspicion in town—it has been reported to the police—that the yellow lines now spreading across the surface of our local ponds come from paint, not spilled accidentally by some sloppy house painter but by vandals. You can also find it covering pools after it rains, coating porch floors, and invading living rooms, to the exasperation of their owners.

Pine pollen is not known to cause hay fever, though many are convinced that it does. Some people are almost as alarmed as they were a few years back when the gypsy moths were chewing up oak leaves in one of their periodic invasions. It was said that our children were endangered, for reasons that were far from clear. We did the children far more potential harm by dousing the town with thousands of dollars worth of pesticides, at a time when the gypsy moths were reaching the end of their population cycle in any case. The following spring there were those who attributed the brilliant green of the grass and the foliage to the fact that they had been sprayed the previous year, diminishing nature's role to a wonderful degree.

Despite contemporary myth and madness, the yellow wind still belongs to our world, to sex and attachment, breath and continuance. If you can make that difficult stretch between hearsay and the tree standing right next to you, then there is a visible reason for it. The male cones on a pitch pine, which develop as numerous small catkinlike clusters, produce the pollen they let loose in May. Each grain is minute, visible through a high-powered microscope, being about one-twentieth of a millimeter, and it is a geometrical figure, crystalline in shape. This dust of golden spores is released on the wind, which carries it for great distances, in forested regions for hundreds of miles. The purpose of each grain, a messenger of heredity, carrying chromosomes, is to reach the female egg in a female cone, which starts off as a little rose-red blossom, to develop the following year into a slim, light green, tapered structure covered with studs, and usually growing on the upper branches of a tree. This cone opens to receive the pollen in the spring, then closes again, but the spores that enter it do not fertilize the egg cells for thirteen months, so as to result in a mature seed. After that the cone becomes brown and woody, maturing at three years and ready to release its seeds. Exceptionally hot weather or an occasional fire will hasten the process. (The pitch pine itself is resistant to fire.)

The little male cones drop off in a few weeks, sooner in open sunlight than in shade. The tide of fertility they release is so extravagant as to be past counting, and most of the pollen grains never reach their destination. In more advanced plants the sexual cell of the male is enclosed within grains designed to be transported, but the pitch pine sends its pollen particles out on the wind and they reach the female organs by luck.

This incredibly ancient method has been called primitive by

a popular theory of evolution that thinks in terms of a progression toward increasingly complex and less haphazard ways of doing things. At the same time, the yellow wind blows from origins we can only conceive of. Other plants employ endlessly ingenious and complicated means to the same ends, but that fierce spending in a pitch pine has the original voice which the human mind has not yet evaluated. And why should not the world have *started* in complexity?

Nature's inspired provisions for regeneration are on a scale that we may be trying unconsciously to reduce, in order to save us from its implications. Sacrifice, not only in pollen grains, or in the vast number of marine organisms that make up the food of the sea, but in all life, is the rule. Thousands of warblers die during the spring migration. The normal mortality of young terns, without the factor of human interference, is 80 percent. Of 80,000 eggs produced by a single female alewife only one hatchling may survive to leave the spawning grounds for the sea. Here is what N. B. Marshall says, in his *Life of Fishes*, about the chances of a mackerel in the marine world: "South of Cape Cod, the catches of eggs in 1932 indicated that some sixty-four million million eggs were produced by a spawning population composed of one thousand million mackerel. During most of the larval life, the mortality was estimated to be 10 or 14 percent each day, but was considerably more (30 to 45 percent each day) in larvae measuring from eight to ten millimeters, at which stage they were rapidly acquiring their fins. By the time the young mackerel were about 50 millimeters long and about to end their planktonic existence, something of the order of one to ten fish had survived from each million of eggs that were laid."

Although we depend on it for our very being, it is hard at times to see the vast expenditure in nature as much more than cruel and unnecessary waste, and we see ourselves in its victims. Why should the dead tern chick, or the trembling baby rabbit lost from its mother, or a cub seal dying of internal injuries, not have been given its chance? Why the terrible anonymity? It might seem unendurable that unnumbered innocents should be born into a world that promises them nothing but abandonment. The earth has a savage heart, and that which nearly matches it is a wayward savagery in ourselves. But who can run away from the great terms of existence and survive in spirit? If I can move one essential step further toward that universal capacity, even in fear, then my life may gain in something more than an isolated sense of itself. "Va com Deus" ("Go with God"), said the Portuguese captains, as the men lowered away in their fishing dories from the ship's side. It is well to honor the dignity of fate as we set out.

For all our dam building against nature, we can hardly avoid sensing its inevitable processes in ourselves. We know that the artificial lengthening of our days fails to cheat death. We know that nothing stops deterioration in our bodies or our machines. What else could bring us, all the same, to mutual love and need, but this universal inclusion? Love your neighbor so as to share mortality. Accept the endless eggs and seeds for their immortal habit, in which we are equals with the frogs, the flies, the plankton, and the pine. No life under the sun is inferior to that of the human species. All have to prove themselves. Who is going to ride out this storm but all its riders?

I go back to the great seasonal passages again, which is inevitable for someone who has lived with their variety for so many years. The seasons have to turn into something more than the four quarters, or how should we recognize their freshness in ourselves? They always predict an entire change. All life pivots on their tidal moods.

One year, on another day when the last of winter seemed to be behind us, I watched the sky curdling, heard the wind picking up, and saw a few snowflakes running before it. According to the radio, offshore winds were blowing at twenty to thirty knots, and small-craft warnings were in effect. In a few hours a tree-cracking wind was having its bold, free way, and I drove off to watch the waves on the outer shore. When I reached it, a green and white surf was boiling along fifty miles of the great beach. The waves had been turned into spume-choked flanks of water heaving back and forth, churning up massive volumes of sand.

The wind stung my face with driven sand and my eyeballs with sleet. The surf munched and licked away at the base of the sandy cliff where I stood, and in one place a crack started to appear. Then a whole section slumped, slid down, and fell away, to be transported by the currents along the shore. Where low dunes, rather than cliffs, confront the sea, the surf sweeps up their face, falls back, does it time and time again, eroding and reducing them, so that the top of the foredunes, which usually make an overhanging bank, are incorporated into the downward-sloping beach itself, resulting in a long, steep profile. In some areas, storm waves cut through these dunes into the marshes behind them.

I returned after a night of booming depths running riot along the shore, with salt spray being cast from one side of the Cape Cod peninsula to the other. Though the storm had begun to slacken, there were sudden explosions along miles of white surf. As the tide retreated, froth from the waves leaped across wet, dark sands. Higher up on the beach, sand grains of white quartz went whizzing and bouncing away. Great combers rose offshore. The surf still sounded like a hundred Niagaras. Sheets of foam ran toward me where I walked, and chased me up a dune.

Out of that cold belly came a sound I had heard before, a commandeering eloquence. A unilateral passion filled the atmosphere and rose beyond the horizon with the clouds. Under the mottled sky, with this great roaring beside me, I felt my tentative existence. I was no more than a jellyfish, a bryozoan or a hydroid attached to ribbons and stems of sea-weed broken off by the waves, fragile laces of the sea. I was no more than a splinter of light struck off coldly silver and sulphurous waves. I raced back and forth with gulls beyond the surf. I was broken like the chunky, black and white body of a dovekie, or little auk, which I found half-buried in the sand. That roaring, loaded tumult could have pulled me in for good; but I knew that it was the right space, the only proportion to define the human spirit. Man's "divorce from his roots" is a terrible deceit. We have nothing less to fall back on, to live for, than this conflict in sublimity, which includes all races, all cellular communities, there being no special guarantee for Homo sapiens. I saw this—praise be—in the grandeur of the caved Atlantic.

CHAPTER 14

Listening

*A*fter we landed on these shores, the nearly constant proximity of birds enchanted me, though it took me some time to hear their calls as a nonverbal speech, rather than as mere background music. When the songbirds moved in waves into the surrounding woodlands in the spring, to court and sing, it simply fitted the characteristics of a season that returned on schedule the way we expected it to. It did not occur to me at first that they were not singing just for the sake of it but that it had a meaning for them. So, with a little more exposure to their realities, I started to listen harder, as, in a sense, I had been listening to the silence of migratory fish.

When Herman Melville wrote *Moby-Dick*, he was not aware of the underwater communication of whales, which does not make his statement about the majesty of their silence less relevant: ". . . seldom have I known any profound being that had anything to say in this world, unless forced to stammer out something by way of making a living." It does look as if our ideas of what is of the most value to us in nature were primarily confined to matters of food and utility; so you have to suppose that we are missing something more important, or at the very least being inattentive to it.

We suppress too many of the sensory tools we need to counterbalance that artificiality which takes so many manufactured tools to maintain. At an early age, those senses for survival so vital to all other animals are stifled in us and later nearly atrophied for lack of use. Conscious prohibitions take over, about the use of our hands, our sense of touch; and what we listen to besides the immediate company is the human voice scrambled, rendered, and returned in unconscionable volume. The noise level of machines in the background is so constant in most places that little else comes through, or is given much importance if it does. In other words, we do not need a bird cry to alert us, or the deep cough of a leopard. We have become, above all, creatures of sight who go through the landscape without enough native equipment to interpret it in any but its more subdued and altered state. We lose the instinctive grasp of what the earth is saying to us in its varied eloquence. Education, a new leading out, so as to bridge the gap between the ear and the song, the hand and the objects of its touch, the sense of smell and its natural choices, is perhaps the best we can do, but we have an extreme deprivation to overcome. We ought to be tuning up to what is around us, but our own static is too loud.

Instead of looking out and listening, which was our original need, we have our heads planted in a television set for much of our lives, and whether we will be able to find ourselves there seems doubtful. Television is a product of our conquest of nature, or to put it in a better light, it is a magic symbol of the conquest of loneliness, the awful prospect of not having any companion but your own thoughts; though I think television watching is in some ways a lonely occupation. Barn raising, feasts, dances, berry picking, gabbing "down to the store," clamming, and calling on the neighbors were more sociable. There is something about the attention we give to the machine that is abstracted and attenuated, like the airwaves it employs.

Here we are in our great indoors while the wild stars fling out beyond us. We are able to abide the weather unless the electricity or fuel give out, when we may expect violence, and we are provided with enough goods so as to be able to have Christmas at home many times during the year.

In the midst of these acerbic thoughts I am interrupted by the clamor of Canada geese, bugling on the outside of my inner ear. They may be warning me of eternity. I run out of the house and dimly see three wedges of them flying over, sounding their great gabbling calls as if from the frontier of another world.

Surely we shield our ourselves from too much real, nocturnal information, as if afraid that the immense darkness might enter and overwhelm us. What would we do with the auora borealis on the living-room wall? Hunger out of cosmic nowhere could turn a man into a mouse.

Still the spring birds consistently call around us, and are later succeeded by locusts, grasshoppers, and crickets, out of a reservoir of sound, of intonation, pitch, and emphasis more complicated in its makeup than the product of any instrument or set of instruments we can devise. I think that by starting to listen, even if we do not come much closer to relating to other languages in the process, we have a chance to rejoin the cycles of universal expression.

There is a dry field below our house, really a double hollow scooped out of the glacial moraine, with two adjoining bottoms, their slopes tilting up toward a ring of oaks, and it is covered with wire grass and bluestem, and patches of sweet fern and huckleberry. Luminous gray-green deer moss lies over it too, in clouds. At one time, I took a young ornithologist from the Cape Cod Museum of Natural History there, and we spent half an hour tracing and identifying a field sparrow that led us in circles with its climbing notes, until we finally spotted it against the dazzling sunlight, perched on a wild cherry, acting like the one and only claimant of that dizzy, aromatic field.

It is a field I have gone back to many times so as to listen to languages I cannot speak. Through practice, though not always with confidence, I have learned to identify white-throated sparrows, black and white warblers, yellowthroats, towhees, and others through their voices. In a few instances, I have learned to identify an alarm call or a territorial song fairly readily, though I have a long way to go. At times I fancy they are just singing in praise of the light, or congratulating themselves on having arrived. It moves me, in any case, to hear a singing speech that has resounded on earth's tympanum for such an incredible length of time. It becomes a mystic form of communication, though real enough. If a bird's pure voice may now be keeping up with the moods and motions of the planet better than I can, then I feel nothing but jealousy toward it.

When a wood thrush sings out of the evening trees, I go back to where I first heard the spiraling notes of hermit thrushes and veeries coming out of the white pines and birches bordering Lake Sunapee in New Hampshire. They gave us and our land a grace abounding. Their freshness is the same as it ever was, though their numbers seem to be dwindling, and it comes out of principles of harmony that we are as much dependent on as they are. Why should the song of a thrush be beautiful to us? In the first place, because we still have earth ears. Also, it takes the path of beauty, avoiding repetition and monotony, following the painstaking traditions of nature with such purity. Our emotions respond because we are there too, as more conscious creators, but never ranging so far from the deeper requirements of form that we are not aware of disorder when it occurs.

Those rippling, half-slurred, vaulted notes are not disembodied. They come out of feeling, live emotion. It seems that for many birds out in the open spaces, sight tends to be more important in signaling and recognition than sound. Many ducks, for example, can see each other plainly across open water, and a "quack" will do. But song may become more elaborate in the region of dense trees, where visibility is relatively poor. Thrushes in the forest engage in "advertising songs" to announce their presence. If a singing male is threatened by a rival thrush, intruding into its territory, it will sing louder so as to increase the "escape drive" in the other until it flies off. This may also result in the two of them engaging in competitive singing for a while, each trying to outdo the other. They engage in a kind of countersinging, which gets more and more intense and elaborate until one bird loses, so to speak, and flies off through the trees, though this occasionally ends in a fight, usually no more than a brief flurry on the ground.

Knowing that the beauty of their song is in part a matter of competition certainly does not spoil my enjoyment of it. I hear the thrushes as even bolder in their ardor and formality than I had realized, and in their intensity they seem to be competing, not only with each other, but with the rest of the singing world, calling out the kind of standards every serious musician understands. There is no backing away from performance.

Carl Jung wrote: "I regard behavior as a mere husk that conceals the living substance within." So what language should we know that corresponds to living substance? I hear it in thrush music through the convoluted chambers of my skull.

The closeness of birds to the light is very marked at dawn, when many kinds sing together. On the other hand, a chuck-will's-widow prefers moonlight. The ovenbird's flight song sounds in the evening, and the mockingbird frequently sings all night, when encouraged by the moon.

"At twilight," says Roger Pasquier in his *Watching Birds*, "the Eastern Wood Peewee sings a faster and more complex song than the familiar whistle given all through the day. Other birds have songs given only before dawn."

"Little work," he then writes in a tantalizing fashion, "has been done on whether the less frequently heard songs have meanings different from those the bird sings all day."

Whipporwills sing—*shout* seems more appropriate if you hear them through an open window at night—in response to the amount of light, like the woodcock, which starts its first evening call, according to William Sheldon's *Book of the American Woodcock*, when the light is on the average of ".71 plus or minus .26 foot candles." For three years, for whatever it is worth, I have marked down the date when I first heard a whippoorwill, and I find that it happened twice on April 24 and once on May 1, another example of hemispheric timing that never ceases to surprise me.

One evening there was still enough dim light that I could just make out a whippoorwill where it perched, or crouched on its short legs, along a rock above the garden wall, looking like a piece of driftwood on the beach. It gave out a loud, shrieking "whip!" before the "poorwill," and with each shriek its head jerked back violently. Since this performance is often repeated hundreds of times in succession, the apparent effort the bird had to make was surprising, unless I am judging it too much by the vertebrae in my own neck, which are poorly equipped for such an exercise. When it became aware of me it flew up quickly and silently like a great moth, a white necklace and a white patch on the tail showing distinctly against the gathering darkness. The time was ten minutes to nine.

Each spring a ring of whippoorwills makes a loud and unrelenting clamor outside our house, and their wild, woodland mating call has always seemed as extravagant as ancient tribes howling under the blood of the moon. I have spent some wakeful hours counting these calls, and until recently, I was jealous of the naturalist John Burroughs's record of hearing a whippoorwill repeat itself 1,088 times. But one predawn I was awakened by a shrieking just outside the window and got out of bed to throw a stick in its direction. That worked for a few minutes, but the same bird, or another one, started up again at close range. Struggling to keep my sleepy head clear, and using my fingers for the hundred marks, I started counting, and this master shouter finally quit at 1,136, with no interruptions between phrases.

With this achievement behind me, I turned on the light to look at my watch. It was about five minutes past four and growing lighter, though the sun would not appear over the horizon until an hour later, this being the end of May. I heard another whippoorwill calling in the distance, but only for a few minutes. Then the passionate white light began to produce more responses: the rat-a-tat voice of a crow, then a catbird's chips, warbles, and scratchy notes, followed by the cheerful whistling of a tufted titmouse, and then the tin-horn sound of a blue jay. This celebration of the dawn took only about ten to fifteen minutes, and was followed by a period of relative silence while life prepared for the next wave and intensity of light.

The whippoorwill calls in its strange style out of some racial relationship with a chosen shade of darkness. It proclaims and hides at the same time, while the woodcock chooses an open clearing and stakes it out for nesting territory, launches mating flights, pitches tents, and raises flags. Its performance, like the whippoorwill's, is in accordance with the motions of the earth with respect to the sun, and takes place on the fringes of day and night. These ritualists attract me out, after supper at woodcock time, when the light is between 5.0 and 0.2 foot candles. Walking down from our little hill, following an overgrown cart track, I reach a bottom land covered with thick grasses growing in a grove of locust trees, and there I have been able to wait and listen for them for many years.. At times I have seen deer there as they bounded off through the trees toward a neighboring swamp, their white tails flashing.

About 8:15 of an April evening, with the light fading, I have often heard a woodcock ahead of me in the grasses, starting to sound its "peent," or what I have heard of as a nasal "zzamp." Then a small body comes hurtling low across the open ground, on a short flight, calling with a kind of buzzy snort, perhaps in warning to another bird. After about fifty peents, the first woodcock suddenly rises up on a slanting course through the dim light and commences to climb, hurtling up like a little whirling projectile, making twittery, warbling sounds. It loops off in one direction and then turns, making a spiraling hook as it goes, reaching a zenith at several hundred feet, to whip down toward the ground, with a "chip-chip chop-chop-chee" that sounds somewhat like the fast dripping of water in a well or underground cavern. It is the male who puts on this show, and I can only suppose that there is a female waiting down in the grass in silent admiration, unless she is suggesting that he ought to try it again: "Just another hundred feet." But it may not be the male's prowess that impresses her so much as his choice of the one and only nesting site. All the concentration and intensity that they put into these courtship flights go to that end, which, in terms of its earth ties, is a sacred one.

The home grounds are still being attached and rightfully employed. The woodcock's twittering and blurting in the fields is an event I can look forward to so as to renew my own sense of the appropriate. I am astonished by whatever it is in that little being that could have such miraculous properties of touch with relation to the great world surrounding it. These often faintly heard, little-noticed reactions to the finest emanations from cosmic surroundings are in everything we too could be, everything we attempt. The power in it tempts us as much into conquest as receptivity. The mind that is able to track light-years out of sight goes with a will to defeat circumstances. And so we fail, time and time again. Human supremacy conquers itself.

Still, the old rituals prevail, holding past and future in themselves. Birds are still following them, while we threaten ourselves with exile. In a time-honored sense, they have as much right to the land as we do. They are ancestral claimants, with a profound sense of direction and internal ties to their natal sites. By comparison, we have almost abandoned the land and the lessons of birth and growth it can teach us. Our local history has become vulnerable, temporary, easily swept aside.

There is an eighteenth-century cottage near these mating grounds, now caving in, a roof with a sky view. It is sinking and sliding down in broken glass, wet plaster, rotten wood and leather, rusty nails, and old mason jars. An iron bed stands in one corner, with its rust-colored legs poking through what is left of the floor. You can hardly hear the human voices any longer. Local memories are losing their hold. But the woodcocks come in to identify the land, whose underlying wisdom survives. Nothing quite erases the tremendous, unseen energy of cognition.

CHAPTER 15

Passion and Vulnerability

The dark, matted marshes lie open, prostrate and torn, with their coarse grasses expressing raw strength under the ripping winds and the enveloping tides. The season gradually delivers them and they start to grow again. In out of the ocean waters and the long shores winding down to the southern continent, in out of wild snow squalls, sun spearing through mountainous clouds, water spouts and rain, low-lying mists, thick fog, and that brilliant light free again to ripen the waters, they drift in crying.

The end of April and early May is the time to look for them, black-capped, gray and white birds with sickle-shaped wings. They float across the marshes and down channels and inlets, veering to the side, skimming, rising and hovering, plummeting in after small fish, all in a tense and lilting style. There is nothing quite like the sure and buoyant flight of a tern. It is flight pared down to its most swift and skillful, its most tempered and pliable motion.

Their voices do not make sweet music like that of a bluebird or a thrush, but have rasping edges. They are shrill, vibrato, with an often querulous tone to them. "Keearrh!" or "Ayhunnh" and "Kip-kip" ring their changes against the complementary tones of the beach grasses, blue water, and sand.

After they first appear inshore, they do not settle down right away on their nesting sites. They have practices to attend to such as courting, pairing up, making preliminary nest scrapes in the sandy ground, a process that takes some days. More and more of them gradually gather at their breeding islands, or low dune areas at the shore edge of a salt marsh, but they may spend their nights away for some days before settling in to nest for good. Courting birds engage in beautifully taut and skillful maneuvers, fluttering together in pairs, or threes and fours, high in the air, or rapidly crisscrossing over and under one another, then easily switching wingbeats from slow and deliberate to wildly fast. They swing together like champions, in an incomparably balanced way, the males trying to draw the females down to the ground, where after long glides, they level off. All the while, they cry out, their vibrant, grating calls having all sorts of variations in intonation, an emotionally accented speech that is hardly ever stilled, even at night.

As the days go by, they change more markedly from the flocking, fishing relationship that governs them the rest of the year, and separate into individual, busily occupied pairs, making their nest scrapes in the sand, then laying their eggs, brooding them, and sharing after they are hatched in the rearing of their violently demanding young.

The terns are "territorialists" in the same sense as herring gulls or muskrats, finding appropriate places on the earth's surface to rear their young and defend them. They also seem to be possessed of a kind of pure anger to carry them through the process, as if it were not nest and young only that they defended but a passionate and fragile quality in themselves and its relationship to earth and its attrition. They are like bird arrows, thrusting into the sea light to search and try again.

The ritualizing among terns is "stereotyped." The same circling, bowing, and neck craning on the ground, the same swinging flights are annually repeated. There is a scientific sense in which rituals of this kind are vestigial, that is to say, they are functional movements no longer existing in terms of their original purpose. We do not know where in bird history they started. But they are one of the arts of the planet, out of original form and the trials of form. It seemed to me as I watched their "fish flights," in which, with or without a silver minnow in their bills, they lead and furiously chase each other, or swing in their sky arcs, that these exercises did not illustrate that stiff term "adaptation" so much as a still spontaneous reaching into the unfinished state of things.

A pair that had mated the previous year and met each other before or after arrival settled in fairly readily without prolonged courtship. Many more spent days at it, with any number of false leads, breaking off, starting again, until the bond was formed between a pair and between them and their little part of earth, a mere scrape in the sand. This indirection, this trying out, reminded me of the circling of alewives finding their way in to their home streams. Their motions were not just fixed. They allowed for open ends. They were flexible enough to provide a possibility for terns to shift territories, move out, change mates, nest again in the face of losses—in other words, to meet new situations.

Behind this, behind all the repeated, ardent effort in the early stages of courtship, and in fact their time on the breeding grounds, was that hidden though figured dimension that life called out in them, a life of high order, fashioned to meet with chance and conditions of unending magnitude.

Terns are agitated and often quarrelsome birds, continually aware of each other's actions, like individuals who have to live close by each other and at the same time find it unnerving. For a large part of the year they fly communally and freely over open waters hunting for fish, but here, where to create new life is a necessity, they become individuals who barely tolerate one another as each pair protects its own nest.

There might be little sense in attributing love or hate to them as we know it, but that they act on poles of feeling is clear. And if you let yourself fall victim to your anthropomorphic tendencies, as I frequently do, at times intentionally, then you can hear all kinds of love or protective cries, cries of distress, anger, and fear. When I first visited one of their colonies, out on a sand spit at the far edge of a salt marsh, I felt as if I were being introduced to a pageant of animal energy, arranging, distributing, finding itself again in earth's centrality. The birds were constantly acting out their involvement, a shrill, excitable crew, begging and protesting all the way.

One day I returned to the colony, walking over the marsh at low tide to reach it, and found that a spring storm the day before had sent seething water over the low dunes into the bare hollows and hummocks behind them. Many nests in the more low-lying areas were inundated. Eggs had been washed out and were either broken or lying around out on the beach. When I got there a helicopter was buzzing by overhead and sending the birds up in a milling flock. I became highly conscious of their vulnerability. Still, unless they desert the premises entirely, which they occasionally do, they tend to rise in the face of threats and ruinous occasions with their usual enthusiasm.

As I came closer to the colony, males with nests on its periphery began to fly at me, making harsh, ratchety cries, and dove at my head. There was a cracking, glass-shattering edge to their voices, a tone of childish, excited anger. This is a spontaneous racial habit that has the effect of distracting intruders from their nests, and to be expected by those who work among terns, but it had a direct effect on me. I was particularly exasperated at one aggressive bird who kept dive-bombing me, time and time again. I ducked. I swore. I retreated. After all, emotional attacks are designed to attract emotion. As I walked away with the terns still screaming and diving at my head, I realized that there was a sense in which they could be said to know their man.

After I and the helicopter had let them alone again, they settled down on their nests. From a distance the colony sounded like a whirring loom. A few pair, perhaps late arrivals, or younger, unmated birds made their skipping flights down an inlet that cut through the marsh, or performed their graceful courtship flights in the air. I thought of terns as gyroscopes for the planet.

They beg, steal from each other, protest, fly up in a nervous, at times silent excitement, and return. Their every gesture seems importunate. The tension you see and feel in their flights is characteristic of much of their behavior; they are spontaneous beings with a short span of attention. If you watch them long enough, you begin to see individual traits. One spends a great deal of time minding its neighbor's business and getting into trouble. Another keeps its distance. Some are clearly more negligent of their duties at the nest than others who are exceptionally devoted, busy, and attentive to its needs. So individual qualities come into view, while the colony as a whole has to concentrate on nurture as if it were on fire.

In the face of a tern's persistence—they often renest after their nests are destroyed—the disasters that come their way can be disheartening, even when you realize that this is the way things are. Storms wash out eggs and nests; foxes eat eggs, as do gulls that prey on unprotected nests. Both young and adults may be attacked and eaten by hawks and owls. Their habitats are taken away from them by gulls and men, and the waters where they dive for fish may be polluted by waste chemicals and gradually affect their ability to breed. Everything seems to conspire against them.

Even under the most favorable circumstances, only a small minority of their dancing, constantly hungry, and demanding chicks, with their gaping bills and agitated cries: "aggh-aggh-aggh," will live to fly away at the end of the season. But they are vehemently answered by their parents. There is no greater danger to a young tern than starvation, and when I saw how intensely this was faced by the adults as they shared in flying out and bringing back food, hour after hour, it moved me, as any acts of selfless devotion can move us. "Give to me!" cry the chicks, "I want! I want!"—which is as vital a cry as any we will ever hear, a challenge to all privation. The terns can never let up. Just to say that they hang on a perilous margin of existence is only half the story. They would not admit their subjection if they were capable of answering you, nor would we for the most part, though our society spends a vast amount of its substance in an insanely exaggerated battle for security. The beautiful thing is the whole effort they put into playing out, with such vehemence and grace, the role that was given them.

Granted the transcendental understanding which encourages us in our role of planetary supervisors, these others are so directly engaged as to shame us. A race that can isolate people in their own compartments, fragment its social entities, and turns to violence, rage, and fear as a result of an imbalanced relationship with an earth it presumes to conquer has a great deal to learn from the terns. Those little birds may seem small-brained, restricted in their vision, and narrow in their range of choice, but comparisons are odious. After all, they are engaged in vital work toward exalted ends in the places best suited to them. Their communities are open to earth's influences. They have a give-and-take direct exchange with it and with their own members, and this is the essence of stability for any society. The risk to them is inherent, as it is for all other creatures. The risk for us is to exclude them.

The arrow bird hovers over the water and makes a quick pitch in, coming up with a small, silvery fish. It has the skill of all fishing people, and of any number of other lives that fly in, swim out, reach for their fulfillment, and die in a minute or a year, being, for all they know, immortally bound. The sun-braided waters sway along the shore, and they carry a depth of response we can only sense. Intricacies of force are embodied in battalions of fish, legions of worms, droves of snails, minute organisms making their daily, vertical migrations through the waters of the sea, up toward the light and down again, scuttling crabs, shorebirds that never rest from feeding and moving on, eternally alert. This is the way creation itself reveals its excellent measures day after day, hour after hour, to tease our freely roaming eyes to follow after.

CHAPTER 16

A Season for Swallows

*A*ny new arrival, any little bird landing in a tree at dusk, has come to seem immeasurably important to me because of the unknown dimensions it brings with it. Who knows what it has seen, or what great risks it has taken? It is a true interpreter of the times. If I ignore or dismiss it, I may lose some of my own precarious footing in the hemisphere. In some of its attributes it is more sensitive to direct messages from the universe than I am. It may have experienced some major phenomenon, some change of global importance, while I was reading the newspaper.

I see no reason to suppose that in the life of my "sister swallow," to use Shelley's lovely phrase, there may not be any number of tangential lines to my own experience, any number of encounters I could share in. Though she lacks my language and my much advertised brain, she is a world being, tied to all worlds, and has as much right to center stage as any of us. The living earth honors its true receivers as much as those who attempt its mastery, and equips them accordingly. We do not live on a one-way street. (If the swallow, like the sparrow, is under the all-seeing eye of God, then neither of us can be said to suffer from neglect.)

So I have yearned impossibly to follow the far-flying swallows the year around, from South to North and back again, so as to see what exactions they have to endure, what hairbreadth hemispheric escapes they make, the degree to which their journeys relate to the constellations, the circulation of the atmosphere, earth's landmarks, and magnetism. This means flying with them, and clearly, I'll never make it, any more than I can get inside a bird's strange being; though it has to be said that if you don't trust some of your own impossible impulses you may never migrate very far yourself.

Before spending another summer in Maine, I went up early, toward the end of April, in order to dig a vegetable garden. There is a small barn close by the house where in previous years barn and cliff swallows had nested in the loft along the rafters, but they were past due when I arrived. Our neighbor told me that a few pair had been flying in and out of her toolshed, but were not satisfied with it as a place to nest. "Nervous about it" was the way she put it. Their problem was lack of access to the barn. They had been coming in each spring through some broken holes in the glass of two old window frames high on the north end, but I had boarded those up in the autumn.

So I climbed up into the loft and took out the boards, and almost at once, as I was climbing down again, four barn swallows flew in, filling the barn with their warbly chatter. A whole new realm of talk and feeling had moved in, a world that in spite of all the years I had watched the passing swallows was largely unknown to me. What were all these low buzzy sounds and higher twitterings all about? Did they have to do with claiming territory, urging each other on to nest, irritation at my presence, or simply the satisfaction of having arrived? In any case it was a pleasure to listen to, like the talk of some cheerful and urgent company moving in on a person who has been too long alone.

These four, with their tribal talk, were of a race that can travel all the way from the latitude of the Yukon to Brazil or Argentina. Their return to the nesting places where they grew up, or where they nested before, ties immense distances together. As it is with the terns, thousands of miles of directive knowledge and memory are in those little frames that can home in on a few yards of territory.

When I let the swallows in I felt as if I had let in earth's hunger. I had relieved some of the pressures of primary need, and at the same time I was struck with how much we block out. It is not only a matter of our overwhelming ability to destroy life, but the extent to which we do not allow it to materialize. The boards against the window are of our own manufacture, which may have all kinds of implications about the human dilemma and the pity of it, but, more important, we should not forget to take them off when it is time.

When we got back there, toward the end of June, the earth was burning. The days were loaded with magnificient African heat, making it close and humid along the Atlantic shore, the kind of weather that causes people to complain and threaten one other. This is natural enough. When the earth sweats, boils, and upheaves, should we not feel similar torment in ourselves? The fishing was poor, some said disastrous. It was reported that many dead warblers had been found in the month of June, probably because of an earlier period of unusually cold weather and a resulting lack of food. The heat was interrupted by periods of fog and drizzle. Hours without wind were filled with thousands of midges and mosquitoes. Local existence seemed

punctuated by bursts of pent-up vitality, followed by exhaus-
tion. I woke up, after a night of battling mosquitoes, to listen
to the news—of plane crashes, economic failures, of the cheat-
ers and the cheated, and dire predictions about the future. As
a result of human tampering with the atmosphere, the glaciers
were going to melt and flood our coastal cities. On the other
hand there might be a new ice age. The doomsayers had only
switched their time span, as a result of the awkward and untried
use of geologic periods. We were as confirmed in our fears as
we were two thousand years ago.

"Behold, the Lord maketh the earth empty, and maketh it
waste, and turneth it upside down, and scattereth the inhabitants thereof." (The difference is that the Lord is no longer the
chief culprit, which only adds to the common instinct for mis-
fortune. We have altogether too much to be responsible for.)

By early July, some of the swallows were already fledged
and flying outside or gathering on the wires to roost. They
ordinarily have two broods, and an occasional pair may be
attending to their young as late as the end of August, or even
into September. I watched them close up from inside a window of the house as they lay along the sills in the summer heat,
evidently enjoying it, though they panted with open beaks in
the full glare of the sun's rays. They scratched and picked away
at their feathers. I fancied a sort of glazed, grim look in their
little brown eyes. This was a life directly engaged in the cosmic
business. I was not altogether envious of swallows if they were
as narrowly serious as they appeared to be. On the other hand,
I watched a number of them playing with a feather as it drifted
along the eaves of the barn, picking it up and passing it along
in a way that charmed me. One day too I saw a dead swallow
at the side of the road after it had been hit by a car. Its mate
lingered by it, flying up and around and then alighting next to
the dead one, time and time again, with obvious concern. So
the elements of play, of love and mourning, entered in, and

the birds went on conversing half the day, with their flickering, warbly, wawky phrases ending in little spitting sounds, a sort of "zzzzz."

They flew over land and water, continually darting and swiftly turning, bringing in a daily catch of vast numbers of insects to feed their young. They would occasionally swish by my head in a mild warning as I walked by the barn. Once I saw them fly out to attack a trim, silvery-feathered tern as it flew over the inlet, and it put on a fine show of aerial maneuvers to avoid them, dipping and rising, going into an almost corkscrew flight, spiraling down to the surface of the water.

"Keep in touch. Keep in touch," the swallows seemed to say. All summer long, through light and heavy weather, I heard their voices running on with minor comments of their own. There was a constant urgency to what they did, as there was with the tern colony, as if every passing hour were the last and first. We could empathize with them through the moods of the weather where we trailed along in our own fashion, moving in, staying out, obeying our impulses.

"I guess I'll go home now" drifted over from across the way, or "Come in out of the rain," which was a grandmother talking to her granddaughter, who did as she was told, though she felt that the rain admired her.

(A collaborative understanding runs through all of life's varied motions, which is never quite captured by the human ability to discriminate between its elements. Swallows and grandchildren share in this flowing tide. Knowing no better, they are centered in the earth's variety. On a more sophisticated level, a physicist might say that the innocent human eye only thinks it sees an unending diversity in the color, shape, and motion of things around it, whereas science knows that diversity can deceive. Through the study of orders and relationships, form and pattern can be resolved into elementary simplicities. So the mind seeks out final order, refining, whittling, getting rid of the superfluous, down to the last invisible "quark"; but since infinity remains, and with it our irreducible sense of diversity, so there is not only virtue but wisdom in innocence.)

Now and then a dense fog closed in along the shore. Like Beethoven's "Grosse Fuge," it was made up of the most complicated harmonies, and open to deep deliberations, near meetings, searchings, and interweavings. Over swirling, gushing tidewater sounds, I heard a single "tik" from a songbird. A swallow flitted out of the barn without a sound. There were droplets of water over the webs of spiders, over intricate twigs and branches, and on glass windows they made flowery blooms. Five people stepped into a boat down by the shore and started rowing off into the fog. They moved in one direction and then angled off on another, involved in the general caution and its major slows and complexities.

After they disappeared, I heard the sound of young eiders splashing in the waters of the inlet. The ducklings made high, warbling calls, which were interspersed with grunting, moaning sounds from their female escorts. They gradually moved out on the ebbing tide like little drifting engines, ducking under all the while into rocks and seaweed, probably picking off periwinkles. (The adults prefer larger food items such as mussels.) These sea ducks, nesting on offshore islands, have highly developed homing instincts. At this stage, the young may be getting further strengthened in their sense of locality, moving out some miles from where they were hatched. They are unable to fly until the end of summer, taking sixty days to fledge, after which they begin to move farther out again, among the seaward islands. Over open water a creche of ducklings looks like a brown, rounded clump of moss, and as a boat comes nearer to them they begin to separate, first in a line, if there is time, then scattered out, ducking under to reappear many yards away.

When a dog ran down to the water's edge and barked, one of the adults made a little snort of alarm. These females, some of them mothers, some nonbreeders, began to herd their charges further away from the shoreline. I could hear a satiny, ripping sound as they would occasionally lift and beat their wings.

Those swallows not already feeding their young were brooding their eggs, and finally I heard the chittering squeaks of more hatchlings demanding food, food, food, with wide open beaks and gullets like small pipes. The parents responded, untiringly.

One night a thunderstorm shook the house. I sat up in bed and was almost knocked back again by a tremendous flash of lightning and a cannonade of thunder. The screens fell off some of the windows. Fruit rolled off the shelf and was spread over the kitchen floor. The front door blew open and sheets of rain came in. The family dog was trembling, hearing the power and judgment of the wild. There was a continuous flickering outside, interrupted now and then by a white light that hit like sudden day, and the thunder and lightning struck the sheeted, tidal waters beyond us with a ponderous crash. The swallows too must have been listening to the gods.

Life's relationship to elemental expression escapes research. What is a thunderstorm, to a bird? During an afternoon of hard, driving showers and sudden gusts, with tumbling thunder and freakish lightning, two people were killed while walking out across a breakwater in Rockland. It was in the news the following day. About the time this tragedy occurred, I was listening to the liquid sound of a thrush, during a lull in the galloping storm, when the light had cleared a little. Then, after each cessation of hard rain, followed by an abrupt silence, white-throated sparrows, chickadees, warblers, and finches all sang together.

After mid-July many more swallows, trees as well as barn and cliff, than had been nesting in our barn began to gather on clotheslines or electric wires, still communicating in their flickering voices. If their range of expression is limited, this only seems to add to its intensity. Their common messages have a vital content. Mutual insistence, when it has to do with food, alarm, or a time of migration, concentrates a thousand words.

The month of August wheeled around again. It is named for Caesar Augustus, rather than for some lowlier animal. But it was not so with the Mayans. For them this was the month of the frog, or Uo. The frog, being associated with water, was chosen for that part of the year which was the height of the rainy season; its first day corresponds to August 5 of our year. Water goes deeper than empire.

During a period of ferocious, record heat, the swallows raced outside, hunting insects. Inside the barn, twenty-five fledged young were lined up for shelter, while three others, less able to fly, had moved out of their nests and hopped down from the hayloft to the barn floor. Several days later and they were still there. When adult birds flew by they begged for food in their staccato tones, but they did not seem to be getting any attention. Possibly their parents had abandoned them because of an absence of food or had met with an accident. It was probably the former, because they had died in a day or two and I found several more dead ones on the floor of the loft.

August, a month when nothing succeeds like excess, began to merge and fall away with the night sky where Jupiter and its moons appeared over the horizon. The asters, deep rose, white, and violet, spun their wheels in the changing light, to which some of the salt-marsh plants also responded with cream-colored seeds, and a few maples began to turn red. There was a new quality to existence. During the divine relocation, the seals moved away from offshore rocks, flocks of shorebirds went racing by, egrets appeared to roost with gulls and cormorants, their plumage shining through water-gray light across the coves. Hard showers of white rain hit loping silver waters. Then the sunlight flooded in again, lying deftly over leaves and in long strips across the grass. Cloud banks lifted, and it turned cold and clear.

There was silence in the barn. Outside it, thirty to forty swallows were lined up, chattering in an agitated way like emigrants about to leave for a foreign land. The dark, temporary well of nurture was being left behind. They would flutter, veer, and bend away, leaping off into the circulation that bathed the globe, taking a header, unconscious of casualty, joined in the deeper unconscious of nature. No other event was more momentous.

Now when I look up at swallows, wherever I happen to be, I can locate myself there and in a wider world. And I know the eternally renewable is close by, no matter how far I go. I praise them for their accomplishment thus far, up to the minute. Birth is the thing, the first and lasting mystery. To be born as a small bird means fierce obedience to eternal process, life's conquest of oblivion. Swallows are lessons in supreme closeness, inescapable connections. Love and disaster begain at home.

How will we ever know the earth unless we listen to what these little ones tell us about inextricable ties? Wake up, somnambulists of the human world: you have a journey to take.

CHAPTER 17

Centrality

I have hardly begun to know this country. At this point in my life, somewhat surprised at having reached it, I am still being pulled in to the currents of a major weather I do not fully comprehend. I am half-conscious of unseen Gulf Streams and Labrador Currents that determine my direction. I am a creature of habit, like the migrant birds, but unlike them I am still undecided as to where to go next, not able to act in terms of the distant goals, the millennia of climatic cycles that must be imprinted on my cells. (As a result of denying our own history, we seem to be suffering from a loss of memory.) Yet I continually touch on motions and exchanges that are just at the periphery of my senses and learn of new languages almost every day. At least, this once neglected backwater of a land has opened out, and from station to station I begin to recognize the signals of its abiding space.

The weather roams around us and every element in life practices along with it, fleeing or approaching one new brink or opportunity after another. The reach goes on, and nothing we have to say about the limitations we see, or create on our own, affects the great process. In and out of storms the perishable egg is laid. Through fog and rain, icy or torrid weather, the migratory people keep on moving and exploring. Every life is half a winner, half a risk. We may label them and go away as ignorant as we were before, but their spontaneity leads ahead.

Out over the flats, the great receptive tidal lands, the sea waters recede into the wide blue distance and then rise in again over a long line of sandy shoals to cover the maze of rooted peat banks inshore. The distant roaring sun sends infinities of rays down through curdling and separating clouds. Winds whip the clam digger or the gull. The world of long sea hauls distributes its responsive people. A flock of sea birds rises to its airs. Creatures of quick responses, catch as catch can, they dip their bills into the water, and make drift flights over the waves to pitch away and disappear across the seas like snowflakes, while the bold planet turns.

Fish in a cove rise to meetings with the air and sky; and as the tidewater trickles through the salt marshes, the minnows twitch and scatter in the ditches. A garter snake slides through the spartina grass. Legions of mud snails crawl very slowly over bubbling marsh mud. Ancient plants move into sight in their appropriate time, like the skunk cabbage that sends up spears in late winter, turning into heads of life with tropical stripes. The woodland starflowers making their appearance in the spring are worth a grandstand seat. Though fragile and short-lived, their blossoms celebrate the thunderous polity of the earth.

Waterbugs run under fresh waters with a jerky motion and water striders make dimpled reflections on the surface. A great variety of spiders keep performing their construction magic,

silken strands across a vast divide. The chickadees bang away
at the bark of trees. A crab spider, touched by a twig, throws
its front legs forward and together in a quick freezing, a protective device designed for disguise. Spring peepers proclaim
their loud, cold love in the wetlands of early spring: "De pro-
fundis clamavi!" Barnacles synchronize their feeding with the
cold splash and retreat of the waves. Sanderlings trip forward
on the sands and retreat again, in a rhythmic dance. Have I
not felt transports of pleasure, have I not almost leaped into
the air at feeling these perennial motions!

We know that the energies lodged in the manifestations of
nature, surprising us with their periodic violence, can bury us,
rock over us like a blue iceberg, drown, freeze, and starve us.
We spend our own energies trying to defeat them or employ
them to our own ends. At the same time, it is in us to know
that a central law requires giving as much as taking, adjusting
to the ceremonials of light, adjusting to each other. If some
unregenerate believer in human supremacy should say to me,
in the spirit of a man who once told me we didn't need nature
or its creatures anymore: "You don't belong with them," I
would answer: "I belong where I am received."

Missing a free exchange between us and the waning riches
of the earth, we invoke the wilderness. But this is wilderness
still, in our blood, where the water runs and the leaves are
shaking. This is our only house and its provision. Home is the
universal magnet. Even the wanderer whose only goal is money
on the run requires it sooner or later, feels it as an imperative.
Home is not only our dugout, our room, our building, the
place we need so as to know one another, but it is the center
where hemispheres cross, the winds collide, where world life
has its lodging. Home is the mortal body where opposites meet
and find each other. We could not survive our own anarchy if
life did not insist on affinity. The searching for it never lets
up. There are no neglected corners, in spite of appearances.

No foot of ground goes unexplored, no surface of any tree is not being probed or occupied, no waters go untouched.

"Missing" is my middle name. It took me the better part of a generation to begin to be aware that a plant had the most profound ways of measuring the light of the sun. I followed the migration of alewives back and forth between saltwater to fresh and still have only a beginner's notion of where they might lead me. We search so as to try and join the world in our understanding, but many have found closer and stranger bonds before us. Not long ago some information came my way about alewife connections which I could never have guessed on my own. I knew the freshwater mussel, with its large, dark brown plate of a shell, having found it along stream edges or the muddy and sandy banks of the ponds in the neighborhood. I even opened a shell and tried a bite of the flesh inside, finding it to have the taste of dishwater, next to nothing, in other words; but coons liked them, as I could judge by their tracks. I found out that Demarest Davenport of the University of California had investigated the relationship between these mussels, one species in particular named *Anodonta implicata*, and the alewives. How was it possible?

In the first place, the mass of these fish run in to spawn at the same time that the mussels themselves release their larvae, or *glochidia*, into the water in "shotgun blasts" from their excurrent siphons, evidently timed to the temperature of the water, which is a factor in the appearance of the fish. These glochidia then attach themselves to the fins and tissues of the herring, where they have a parasitic stage of about twenty-one days before dropping off, at a time when their hosts have left their breeding ponds and are heading downstream. The conclusion Dr. Demarest and his colleague, Maryanna Warmouth of Harvard, reached was that though these larvae could be made to attach themselves to other kinds of fish and even tadpoles, their relationship to alewives was species specific. As they put it: ". . . the parasitic stage of *A. implicata* cannot complete its development on the tissue of other fishes to which it can be caused to attach experimentally and, further . . . this stage can be of no greater duration than the time spent in freshwater by an individual alewife." What a perfect advantage for one species to take of another! That this triggering of mussels should occur at all, at that specific time of year when these marine fish visit freshwater, might seem astonishing, if we did not see such balanced timing through the years; it is like hitting a star with an arrow. The symbiotic relationship between alewives and glochidia involves the realm of mutualism, and this is where our own meetings have only just begun.

We may not like the term parasite, or parasitic, but exchange is necessity, even in its most consuming, deteriorating aspects, as with the ticks that drain the blood of a rabbit for their own reproduction and survival. There are parasites in marine mammals, like whales and seals. There are mites in a bird's feathers, parasites in the eyes of a marsh stickleback; fungi grow on the scales of an alewife during a period in fresh water; fungi, benign or destructive, grow on trees. They all ride in the body and tissues of the earth. And we ourselves are hosts to a universe of bacteria.

The common home is alive by reason of all the practitioners who have learned to share it. The human race hardly knows enough so far to discriminate between them, and knows even less the more it disposes of them. Each life, however high or low we put it on our comparative scales, always biased toward ourselves, has its own unequivocal space. There is still time to let them in, so as to relearn what we need. Who knows how many nonaccredited teachers may be lurking in the shadows?

One evening there was talk at a neighbor's house about the scarcity of foxes in town, and the possibility that many might have died of mange, or loss of habitat. As we drove home I saw one by the side of the road. It was a small animal, and as the car headlights struck it, it skipped off lightly between the trees, with a gay, signaling tail that seemed larger than its body.

There was something about the sequence of conversation during the ongoing dark, followed by this appearance, that took on a dreamlike quality, as if the fox were giving me a personal assurance that it lived. "By God, you made it!" I thought, "materializing out of all these grids, these claims that jail the country." Past those who are possessed by possession sneaks the cautious one with its tail.

The only way we will truly know our own country is through a partnership with its upholders, those who by their collaboration have kept it stable for us up to now. There is no use in so much discrimination against them that we fail to respect their basic role in our own future.

One day I came quite close to a downy woodpecker just off the trail as it was extracting what appeared to be an insect or its larva buried in the branch of a shrub. Since it did not fly away from me, I watched it for a while, and then walked over when it had finished, to find a precise little hole, like the one a dentist drills in a tooth. Each to its specialty. I do not credit the downy woodpecker with much brain, but skill, yes, and to watch its carpenterlike operations when it digs larger cavities, making the chips fly in a confident style, is enough to make me think skill may have come before brains and be reconciled to it. Are there not a great many examples of barely conscious life that may be headed in our exalted direction; and are we not continually passed by creatures maneuvering on this earth of conflict and danger with an assurance we often wished we had? The sparkling-eyed, sensate intelligence of a mink, as it hunts the northern shores, is in touch with every message from the world around it. Many others counted slow and stupid are canny in unseen areas.

A great-horned owl does not waste time worrying about its life role. That is a human prerogative. But having a sense of its own unique place in the universal order, it would be entitled to feel that what it is in charge of should not be entrusted to lesser mortals. Senses acute enough to detect mice in their tunnels under the snow, sight and hearing in command of the twilight and the dark, have few equals. Great-horned owls deliver uncompromising messages to the world, and to listen to a pair of them duetting in predawn courtship is to open your dreams to a winter's moon that has been suffering lately from psychic neglect. I once saw one of these savage birds, injured and taking refuge in a thicket, as it was being mobbed by a flock of crows, and its humiliation shocked me, perhaps because I had never imagined before that such pride could be reduced. We do not often see such wreckage in the wild.

These spatial prerogatives are in all things, and the lands they themselves explore come alive through degrees of awareness which can hardly be isolated from our own unless we are to completely deny our origins. I see a wasp, devoid, in our sense, of love or higher intelligence, flicking over the ground like a scientist with a hypothesis. In the complex social behavior and organization of the ants we see our urban selves. The chipmunk and I face our problems in entirely different ways, but we are both endowed with a global curiosity. Terns in courtship offer symbolic worlds to each other. So do we all.

Despite all the dominating distractions of our world, despite those secondary landscapes we keep trying to impose on the original one, we are unable to go it alone. Nothing escapes the rhythm of the tides. Running through the brook, unseen in the air, flowing in the sap of trees and the veins of humankind, in the streaming gardens of the tide pools where the amphipods are swimming, is the immense consanguinity of earth creation, infinitely inventive, infinitely abiding. Collaboration and interchange, in the grasses under our feet, in the soil and surrounding waters, ceremonialized by the smallest under the sun, waits for us too, as beginners who have only started to try out the term "ecology" on our tongues.

On this wayward journey, where I have felt as unredeemably wild as anyone else at just the impossibility of being myself,

I have always been mysteriously restored by an unseen drift during the night, a tide by day. My inward tortures have been concluded by some outer patience, my locked desire released by vast openings like the spring which let nothing elude them. Dreaming or waking, we are creatures of a fire, centrally involved through no fault of our own. That I am in want is earth's prerogative, not mine. I move on and out again through periods of conflict and apprehensiveness only because I am part of what continues after me. This does not imply passivity in the face of the unknown, but the only active participation. The reality never leaves us. The company keeps. It is not because man is unique that we are saved but because uniqueness is a characteristic of all things. The differentiation of my spirit is what gives me personal hope; it exists through supreme complexity, like the flounder at the bottom of the bay. A greater life moves us. We need a revolution toward equality. It is a high distinction just to breathe.

CHAPTER 18

Hunger and the Crickets

Fish, fiddler crabs and barnacles, snails and shrimps measure the tides, while the tides measure the rest of us. The waters begin to recede again toward their rocking plains offshore, and there is no time to lose. The gulls with their half-human screams and mutterings begin to gather on the flats, proclaiming to a windy world. Harshly crying terns scan and interpret the ebbing waters and plummet in to catch their silvery prey.

A flock of sandpipers, restless as the great air itself, swings back and forth over a sandbar beginning to be revealed in the distance. They make the shape of a net that flows like a ribbon and then flings off with the elastic quality of some fine wire whip, then switches direction to level and land, dropping off its little individuals to go scuttling on the bar together. When they fly up again to land along the swash, the scalloped sheet of water that keeps sweeping down the beach after each wave falls back, they act to its rhythms, running down with it and returning, while pecking into the sand for their food, always edging and turning in a manner that shows their senses have been measuring it for millions of years. And when the flock silvers off again in the brilliant light it feels the atmosphere as the fishes feel the sea.

So everything, in the sea or on the land, seizes its opportunity. The seasonal hunger flow on through, putting as much trial and suspense into the birth of field mice and as much fire into the eyes of a chickadee as into any twenty-four-hour watchers like ourselves. We too must keep up to live. Miracles of timing lie ahead.

Where we are, along the shore of all shores, there are supreme standards. What ultimately do we depend on but the leaf and flower buds swelling like a woman in her time, the moving up of grasses and their dying down again, the heron with its blue-mist feathers, who is death to crabs, flying in to a cove being emptied of its waters? Still heat in still trees follows icy rain. Loud water in the brook runs down obedient to the weight of the sea. Clouds move by with images of that dissolution and synthesis which defines the periods of human existence. All things are informed with a power through which we find ourselves again.

There is a field I keep revisiting because it almost careens down to the seawaters below it and far off, so I have an illusion of free travel. At the same time, it sounds with its own multitudes, most of whom, being of the insect tribe, are relatively unknown to me. After it has been left uncut for a while, this field gets overgrown with hardhack, raspberries, thistles, goldenrod, St.-John's-Wort, vetch, milkweed, and other flowers. Its grasses are bent down and molded here and there where deer have rested for the night. Wood-nymph butterflies fly in from the fringe of trees at its head. The fritillary, whose larvae feed on violets, visits it. The monarch, with red-orange wings like slices of a sunset, uses the milkweed to lay its eggs. The stridulators, tappers, hummers, and buzzers form a symphony together. There are spittle bugs, plant hoppers, small flies, and bees from one end of the field to the other. Single dragonflies go hawking over the tops of plants. Beetles probe beneath them. During late summer scarcely an inch of ground in some areas is not covered with the bounding, crawling, and skipping of little brown and black crickets. There are also innumerable sowbugs, also called pill bugs, or armadillos, to be found in the damper ground they prefer, and on the blades of grass other small, delicately green insects wave their antennae and when disturbed sail up and off again to land on other grasses, from which they are inseparable.

There could be no more deeply subtle, delicate forms of interchange between differing forms of life than in the plants and insects. I confess that entomology is one of those branches of science which seems to have eluded me. I put it as much under the heading of natural mystery as of history, but I don't have to travel far through any year to see that the insects preceded me. One spring I stopped long enough to kneel down and look more closely at a lady-slipper, or moccasin flower, a simple act that I had thought about doing for altogether too long. The blossom was a pink, semitranslucent sack, testicular in shape, with sticky hairs inside, and fine white veins whose purpose was to guide a bee into the interior. It smelled a little like raspberry syrup. The lady-slipper puts on a beautiful, brief show so as to attract the insect and detain it in its chamber long enough for it to eat the nectar there, and then tunnel its way out with a little difficulty to the back, where it has to crawl under the flower's stigma, so scraping off a load of pollen. Then the bee flies off to pollinate another lady-slipper. It seems like an elaborate means to attract an associate life, though it works, if sparingly. I saw no bee in the vicinity. On the other hand, I did see some little jumping spiders on the ground next to the flower, and they were evidently waiting in ambush for an unsuspecting victim.

Von Frisch found out that honeybees, which visit raspberry blossoms and goldenrod in that field, can not only signal back the locality of food sources to each other but also remember where they were, so as to return to them later. There is evidently something in the honeybee that is comparable to mental experience. You might suspect that the nervous impulses in the cells of plants, the sensitivity of animals in tide pools, the acute reactions of insects are in no way separable from our own functions, and that they are aspects, like the rays of the sun, of the relative degrees of awareness that are properties of existence. How could the human mind be elevated to the apex of a pyramid and have no connection with the million species of insects at its base? Surely our brains were nurtured by the same universal magic that binds an insect and a flower.

The fact that most insects live for only a few weeks, or even days, and have tiny brains only seems to add to their foreignness and intensely strange character. The devices through which they take advantage of everything from dung to petroleum are incredibly varied, and so are their means of reproduction, which allow for little hesitation in their short span of life. Assassination often accompanies mating. Larvae may devour their mother. From our perspective many of their ways seem sordid, but they are highly successful. The power of mimicry in insects, the walking stick on a twig, the gray moth identical with gray bark, is inspired. The elegant monarch butterfly transformed from a jade pupa shaped like a vial, with a golden collar, is a declaration of universal artistry and desire.

The insects have solved the intricate problems of community living, and they outnumber the rest of us by far, comprising five-sixths of all animal species. Their potential as educators for a new race like Homo sapiens goes largely unadmitted. Their kingdom is anything but neutral, which is one of the reasons that they cause us so much fear and revulsion. We have competitors, but if the competition is in the field of shared awareness then the game may do us some good.

Life in its seasons meanders into sight like a stream, comes up suddenly like a sulphur butterfly. I am not any more prepared than I ever was simply by being able to name it. The metallic blue wasp poised flicking on a leaf has worlds of investigation behind it, but as it gives room to be imagined it is new in me. It materializes out of the brilliant risks of being. The dragonflies and damselflies that come in such wonderful colors, carmen or green in one, glassy sky blue, dazzling lavender in another, fit the earth's wetter places with such innovative perfection as to leave me with nothing wanting. I remember a dragonfly with honeycombed eyes, micalike wings, and a body of granite gray with glints of blue as it came in to land on a rock by lake waters; it added a streak of divinity to it.

There is a decisiveness about some insects that is alarming, as if nature in trying out species with narrow limits and authoritarian functions could ensure their survival better than our freer and more ambiguous ways. One morning, as I was on the telephone next to the front door, I saw a yellowjacket outside, just as it landed on a slim, pale green grasshopper in its nymphal stage, and stung it. Then it proceeded to bite off the victim's head, then chew off the legs and wings like someone with a pair of snips, to fly off finally with the severed abdomen, first circling in the air to get its bearings. The act was performed with such surgical precision, so fiercely and positively, with such vast and ancient authority behind it, that it took my breath away.

There may be in insects no self-determination as we know it, but they are as close to earth's need for alliances as any other life. Once I saw a large moth "making love" to a wild azalea blossom. It was a fox-colored, furry-bodied creature on fast-whirring wings with which it could stand still in the air. I fancied that it half glanced at me as I peered at it, and I was lost in the perfume of the flower, the physical perfection of the moth, the magnetic tie between them both.

The grasses nearby were covered with the foamy nests of spittle bugs, or froghoppers. I robbed one nest of its occupant, a pale tangerine-tan larvae that reminded me of a film I had seen of a kangaroo embryo in its early stages crawling across its mother's pouch. It moved across my thumb, a dry, creased, and barren landscape, with apparent reluctance, halting at the top. Then, not remembering which mass of spittle I had taken it from, I put it on another one, where it disappeared, displaced into the wrong environment, but happier than on my hand. All I know about myself and my unscientific, clumsy meddling is that I do not know where to start. It is lucky that the great arrangements are on hand to start me.

Fireflies pulse across the field on a summer night like little flying saucers, flashes of light, original, cold illumination carried in the lower parts of their abdomens as they deliver a very old message about attraction and risk, the signaling of one sex to another, the need to people the light in its elemental fire.

In the sunlight I sit in the grass and wait for life to act, to jump all over me. It probes, flicks, feels out, scents, calls, darts away, hangs in, hovers on a leaf, a ray of light, all in terrible seriousness. It is not for me to advance the world's knowledge of a fritillary, or cognition in honeybees, but as this company searches, so do I. I sit in the field with the crickets, the grasshoppers, and the lacewings, with the clouds floating by, and I feel the earth moving under us. It is a field of currents like the tidal waters beyond it, full of timeless opportunity. In me are the maelstroms of the human world, wandering apprehensions, unresolved conflicts, and at the same time I am held, contained. Sitting in with crickets I join the unseen depths that motivate us both. I am held in orbit, with the sensing earth. Under the field is another sea of incalculable force, whose energies combine and recombine propagating the reactions of physical and psychic life with incredible speed. Hunger made the human and the cricket. The order that holds us together is irreducible.

I am on my way now to see myself in the wasp, the honeybee in its parallel with my mind, the herring gull in its dominating community. The futility of separation from them has become all too evident. We have to take the risk of whatever future we mutually arrive at, or have more of a future than we can handle on our own.

I think I can say this much, though I am still groping, still probing the darkness of unknowing. The things we do, or fail to do, become more significant as they are involved in the concentricity of the world. You listen best when other lives are listening. Any minor act we take is heightened by the full vigor and engagement of its surroundings. Nothing we say can be completely empty or idle except insofar as it is isolated from an environment that busies itself with us, as we in turn occupy ourselves to its advantage. We become more than we are when there are others than ourselves, whether of foreign speech, or no speech at all, to measure our lives by. We are superior only to the degree that we share superiority. The truth is a composite thing. This new country, this older wilderness that spawned us, exists by reason of the inclusion of infinite force, danger, and opportunity. The only reality is in participation.

CHAPTER 19

Coexistence

A December evening, with a coppery sunset seeping through the kind of smudged and streaky clouds that say rain. There is a flock of dunlins accompanied by a couple of black-bellied plovers on this late migration, probing the wet sands. Squeaks and peeps, faint trilling sounds, come from the little sandpipers as they are busily preoccupied with slipping their decurved bills into the sand and deftly taking them out again. Every now and then, they make aggressive little rushes at each other, aggression in their case having no large territorial implications, only small ones: "Let's keep order. Don't crowd me." So they belong to the family, but the gentle sounds they make, coming over lightly withdrawing waters on the shining flats, seem like extraterrestrial emanations, faintly spiritual, not tied down to much that I can square them off with, or see to a conclusion, standing on the beach in my hard shoes.

That I can tell what birds these are, that I know their names, may be useful to modern man, but it is not enough. They pass me in their restless way, probing the prismatic sands, out in front of the retreating sun. Their cries are secrets of the wider world they follow. They are the tones of a lasting wilderness, accents we will never quite be able to decipher. Science is not enough, neither will any discipline be enough, since each life and its voice is a unique response to universal change. So the old ritualistic speech of the Micmac, the Arapaho or the Cheyenne, and a hundred other tribes, now faintly heard, or not at all, with its individual sounds and intonations, invoked the forces of the great continent where they traveled. They are lost, they are renewed in the living world. Under the communications network through which we call the earth our own, a greater dialogue continues.

I have been down to the shore hundreds, probably thousands of times, and each time I have found it changed. The beach has been cut away, or filled out, or the wind lies differently on the water, but for the most part these changes are not so drastic as to immediately catch your eye; they are a matter of elements that are always reconstituting themselves. And with these elements, resettlements take place. We come in on new territory all the time. We may have thought we owned it, but the ground has shifted under our feet. We have to reorient ourselves, reset the compass, take a fix on the sun, and pay attention to the tides, no matter how many times we have been here before. The great earth does its work on a scale we are unable to tie down; it moves away from our calculations like the water itself. Its great circulatory scheme, in which every life in nature plays an active part, is too complex for human claims. Throughout the changing tides, life in every current and corner adjusts, compensates, and moves on. Mystery is their only proof, forever revisited.

The waters of the living world invade and pass these sands,

bringing transcontinental travelers with them. Here it was that I was first initiated into some of the great ceremonials, the entry of alewives during the spring, the appearance of terns, shore-birds, and songbirds out of the southern hemisphere, the pushing in of arctic ice and its retreat, the passage of whales and seals. It is a moving frontier, exposed to every weather, and involved in a give-and-take relationship with the land and the seas beyond it. No other region on earth is stricter in its biological laws so far as its shore dwellers are concerned, and at the same time rhythmic on the grand scale. It transcends its own boundaries.

A Danish ornithologist once told me, in connection with the political division between East and West, that the terns in those northern regions knew no such arbitrary barriers, any more than the reindeer did on their migrations. They passed the arctic outposts for nuclear defense, the barbed wire on the borders, the searchlights, and the armed sentries. They knew the world not as we do, in terms of dominating cultures that divide spheres of influence between them, but as a continuum, from one curving coastline to another and across the open seas.

Because the terns come back to breeding areas that have been denied them, by gulls or people, conservationists try to save what habitats are left, setting aside protected areas, and it is essential. Without an island, stretch of beach, or dune where they can be relatively undisturbed, they produce no young. But wildlife refuges and sanctuaries isolated from the surrounding world of life and its great distances may be an invitation to sterility. Without access, nurture is impossible, and that is also true of us. A world-dominating society that gives itself and the rest of life no room, no intervening space, is a denial of space, physical and of the spirit, that individuals and civilization need to survive.

The essence of this planetary home is of course recognition and attachment, no matter how far any given migrant may have to travel. And on this beach, or for that matter, on any part of the earth's surface, are living communities that have found appropriate lodging within a vast range of possibilities in which to perpetuate their kind. For them this demanding but receptive place is the center of the world, where life assumes the risk.

During the spring and summer months, in a few separated colonies along the outer beach that faces the Atlantic, least terns, with yellow bills, nest above or close to the high-tide line. They are not as large or as obviously aggressive as their cousins the roseates or the commons, though I have seen them fly after gulls that flew too close to their nests. They sit demurely in their little scrapes over stretches of white sands, well hidden with their gray and white feathers, hardly moving until an intruder blunders or steals in. During the summer months thousands of people occupy the beach. Not far from where these trim little birds are nesting there are parking lots holding hundreds of cars. Least terns are gentle, lovely little birds, of quick and lively flight and with cries that have a tinkling edge like a bell's. There is a certain valiance to their activity, courting in early spring, sitting on their tiny, speckled eggs, feeding their young. If birds can hold their breath, I suppose these do. They live next to a sprawling, noise-making human crowd which is largely oblivious to them, and in addition to human disturbance, which may be held in check by signs and ropes in protected areas, they have to endure the age-old dangers that they have always been exposed to. Storms may wash out their eggs and nests. Great-horned owls and hawks may prey on them. Herons, foxes, and skunks will eat their eggs. Various kinds of predation, however, are seldom permanently concentrated but seem to occur randomly from one season to the next. Whatever happens, chick mortality is high. With luck, 20 percent of them may survive to migrate south at summer's end.

After their first few days of life, tern chicks scatter from the scrapes where they were hatched and take refuge from the heat or intruders in patches of vegetation, or under driftwood. Hard to spot in the first place, they can be almost invisible even as you watch them. But when disturbed, they often take refuge in tracks made by beach buggies. The result, in areas that have not been fenced off, is that chicks may be crushed by passing vehicles, especially at night. Since these vehicles are often driven by people with "rights," such as sports fishermen, or simply those who feel that it is their God-given privilege to drive where they want to, wardens, in an area lucky enough to have them, have to exercise the utmost tact, firmness, and vigilance. Those who labor night and day to watch the nesting birds, make censuses, monitor, and patrol serve as mediators between them and human pressure. Our occupation, added to natural odds, can tip the balance against tern populations, principally because the loss of their nesting habitats is such a crucial factor. How do we, with our rights, learn to compromise?

Having a relatively long life, terns will come back to nest again another year. They will even re-nest during the season if their nests are destroyed early enough. The persistence with which they migrate in to try again in the face of constant attrition might seem inflexible and automatic to us, but it is a need that keeps the worlds of life together. In a sense, these birds are pathfinders for the rest of us. They have an inner, dynamic cognizance of the kind of wild context they need to assure their future. The intensity of the nesting season is woven in to the complexity of the shore. They declare that the beach is not the monopoly of any one species but one of earth's universal properties. The problem of protection is not just a matter of sealing off these birds against all interference, from foxes, owls, or human beings, which is impossible on the face of it, but one of education.

For all the people who are angered that a mere bird should be allowed to get in their way, there are as many who are ready to respect it, if they learn that we share the world. Dennis Minsky, who worked as warden for the Cape Cod National Seashore for several summers, had this to say: "Used to the relative solitude of May and June, when the air was full of the terns' raucous cries, I was never prepared for the bumper-to-bumper traffic, the sky full of myriad kites, the endless procession of volleyball nets, the ubiquitous odor of hamburger on grills, and people, people, people. And so many of them happy to see them, curious about the birds, satisfied that, being outside the posted areas, they were coexisting with the terns, doing no harm.

"And I knew it was not enough."

The process of education is a continued fight against separatism, which can create annihilating barriers that can hardly be recognized until we run into them ourselves. Yet we too are exposed to universal hazard on an open beach. Even in a city of a million souls or more, we are still subject to wilderness laws of chance and attrition, which we experience through the interplay of our common lives. Our hunger and our hope are tested by universal capacity. The cities of birds and the cities of men and women sprang from earth's desire.

We sit out like the terns on the primal sands, subject to forces we never made, taking our chances with survival. The terms of that older wilderness are still the terms of all life on earth. They will not vanish. The only vanishing point will come to us if we go on starving our connections. Cosmic justice denies that there is one law for the human race and another for the rest of life.

The little sandpipers flit away. The terns and the alewives have long since gone. Winter is coming to the beach, where I sit by myself, facing the inevitability of the cold, with the bare rock, rock worn down to nearly irreducible sand fragments, millions and millions of years in arriving, a vast progress measured by earth's passage through the skies. This is the common level, the essential poverty. I have known this range of sand, boulders and stone as a very busy, at times a very lonely place. It endures the continual flooding and backing out of marine waters, the inconstant winds, as well as sleet storms and pack ice, and is periodically exposed to desiccating heat. Its life, like our own, is centered within the great stature of extremes.

Beyond the sands, the granite-gray surfaces of the waves line out, whipped by the wind, while the leaden stream of the outgoing creek reflects a last golden light. Gulls lift and dip down into its waters. While the land begins to hunker down and accommodate to the arctic, the offshore waters protect their passions, keep sending in their signs. I found a fishlike cluster of creamy eggs as I walked down the beach, a little glistening ball I could not identify, left by the tide. Life floats in to prove my ignorance, if that ever needed any proof. But our reaching is never finished. These flat lands are like broad wings, stretching toward the cold sky, beyond the grain of the immediate, worlds without end. What should I do, if there were any choice, but fly?

The harsh flutes of the terns, heightening the windy dunes, cutting through the air, still sound in my ears. What can equal a bird? What can compare with that passionate fiber? Where with all our substitute constructions can we possibly equal that rapt eye, wing quiver, and balance, that sensitive grasp of the earth's whole atmosphere, an instant hunger seizing on the instant? Yet all contrary and sympathetic nature is in human nature. Though we are as uncertain about our mutual relationships as the terns, bonding being an often fragile process, we are sent ahead in greater company, as the flaming coordinates of the sun's rising and setting fix the sides of the world.

As human speech rose from the seas of universal expression,

so there is no human love without nonhuman love. Even our wayward passions are of the earth. We exist in terms of superior changes we never created on our own.

Darkness is moving in and great boulders stand out like monoliths against the sand. We are newcomers to these shores, and have found out little more than that we have infinitely more to know. Any single day, we are on the threshold of discovery. On this side of the world we are being again invaded by an immortal night that has never rendered up its secrets; but it is that experience-in-being which is unable to count its own ends and nonetheless flies off into the future, which is our ultimate resource. The risk is everything.

The cosmic presence whose seas go rocking past is peopled by innumerable beginners in creation. We follow and learn how immensely wide it is, and how far we still have to go. This beach is our original ground, a center of the world. Here is the outward-facing place where human life, even when lost in fear, can declare an entirety, without knowing why.

The name the Navajos gave the First Man in their creation myth was "Anlthtahn-nah-olyah," which means created-from-everything.